SYSTEMS FOR SUCCESS

SYSTEMS FOR SUCCESS:

*The Complete Guide to Selling, Leasing,
Presenting, Negotiating & Serving in
Commercial Real Estate*

By Michael J. Lipsey

With Karen Poirier and Rusty Fischer

PELICAN PUBLISHING COMPANY
GRETNA 2007

First edition, 2003
First Pelican edition, 2007

ISBN 9781589803114

Printed in the United States of America
Published by Pelican Publishing Company, Inc.
1000 Burmaster Street, Gretna, Louisiana 70053

To all my friends, clients and acquaintances in the commercial real

estate industry, you have enriched my life through your generous

association.

TABLE OF CONTENTS

INTRODUCTION: *The Complete Guide to Commercial Real Estate*

PART ONE: *SELLING & LEASING COMMERCIAL REAL ESTATE*

PART TWO: *PRESENTING SKILLS FOR COMMERCIAL REAL ESTATE PRACTITIONERS*

PART THREE: *COMMERCIAL REAL ESTATE NEGOTIATION*

PART FOUR: *SERVING IN COMMERCIAL REAL ESTATE*

Michael J. Lipsey

INTRODUCTION:

The Complete Guide to Commercial Real Estate

If there was ever a single book, one must-have volume, that was absolutely necessary for your office, home, or personal bookshelf, it is *Systems for Success*. Part of the *Systems for Success* line of products, including the new DVD and Field Guide, contained within the pages to follow are the essential skills necessary for success in commercial real estate: **Selling**, **Leasing**, **Presenting**, **Negotiating**, and **Serving**.

By mastering these key disciplines to a greater degree of personal satisfaction, you will finally achieve the success that you've been searching for in our highly competitive and ultimately rewarding field. Whether you're fresh out of your first real estate class or five years from getting your gold watch, *Systems for Success* provides you with just that: Key ingredients to help you learn, grow, achieve, and *succeed* in commercial real estate.

With over twenty-five years of experience selling, leasing, presenting, negotiating, *and* serving solely in the field of commercial real estate, I have tried to distill every lesson learned, every mistake made, and every *success* I've had into these pages. The result is a proven, practical, and entertaining *Systems for Success*.

Wherever possible, I give you the most basic, newsworthy, and timely information encapsulated in Top-10 lists, charts, graphs, and boxes containing the best quotes, one-liners, and "things to remember" from each and every section. Scan forward, browse back, skip over, and return to. Whichever your preferred style of reading, digesting, and remembering, *Systems for Success* was written **by** a busy businessperson **for** the busy businessperson.

In **Part One**: *Selling and Leasing*, I give you the tools you'll need to master this most difficult—and rewarding—aspect of the commercial real estate industry. From "Defining the Ideal Target Market" to "Questioning Skills," I will guide you through the art of selling in easy-to-digest, quick-to-decipher nuggets of worthwhile information that read more like a friendly conversation than a rigid textbook. By the end of this worthwhile chapter, I guarantee that you will feel more confident—and competent—in your salesmanship skills.

In **Part Two**: *Presenting*, we tackle another different aspect of our competitive and high-stakes industry. You'll learn the different types of presentations, from high profile to one-to-one, the latest tools to make your presentations memorable, and tools for following up on your presentations to capitalize on their impact. After this chapter, you'll no longer dread making a presentation to an individual—or a group of 2,000. In fact, you may even begin to look forward to them!

In **Part Three**: *Negotiating*, you will master the fine art of this often-daunting skill. Personal skills meet poker faces in this revealing look at one of the more difficult tasks associated with our industry. With newer, younger, more nimble brokers always competing for your tenants' needs—you'll need the skills presented in this chapter just to compete.

In **Part Four**: *Serving*, I will share with you the ins and outs of customer service, tenant/client retention, and the often challenging art of relationship management. You will discover practical, timely methods to make your tenants happy, renew their leases, and give the most tenant satisfaction per square foot this side of the Taj Mahal!

By the time you are through reading this comprehensive volume, you will possess all of the tools needed to succeed in your chosen profession. The end results are up to you. Applying your own personal work ethic, passion, and drive to the principles learned herein will determine whether this book was a stepping stone—or a pole vault—to your continued success in commercial real estate.

Combined with other key ingredients in the *Systems for Success* line of commercial real estate products, including the DVD series and practical Field Guide for day-to-day use, I wish you the greatest success and happiness in this most worthwhile of professions.

PART ONE:

SELLING & LEASING COMMERCIAL REAL ESTATE

Michael J. Lipsey

Introduction

Great salespeople, like great politicians, teachers, statesmen, and negotiators, are not born—they are made. They may enter this world with inclinations toward brokering a deal or a certain knack for selling someone on an idea—superior people skills, a photographic memory, a great smile—but only with plenty of training, expert tutelage, and even more experience will they ever achieve true greatness.

Like fine wine or profitable stock portfolios, great salespeople improve over time. They learn from their mistakes, earn multiple honorary doctorates in the school of hard knocks, observe the right way to do something, and learn twice as much from watching other people doing it the *wrong* way.

Great salespeople exude confidence, possess terrific skills of persuasion and, above all else, *sell*. But another trait they possess is the driving desire to always, *always* close more deals. All the selling skills in the world won't mean much if you can't close the deal when it's time for the client to put pen to paper.

Taking the art of the deal to new heights, generating the most revenue, the highest commissions, and commanding the most respect is the ultimate goal of each and every great salesperson you emulate, envy, and aspire to. These envied and admired salespeople even have a name—**Top Performers**:

- Top Performers take ownership of their customer's goals and create value by transforming information into new and tangible knowledge for their business.

- Top Performers understand the prospects' vision, values, and core competencies—and provide a new level of participation and collaboration.

- Moreover, the consummate Top Performer employs a highly effective and systematic approach to sales and leasing that is not only calculated and efficient, but positions them as a valuable strategic partner—and their customers take notice.

Our own systematic approach to success in the rapidly evolving field of commercial real estate comprises a simple, logical, 10-step system:

Step 1: Determine Personal Annual Financial Goals and Specialty

Step 2: Determine Activity Ratios (Market Velocity + Personal Skills)

Step 3: Develop a Sales Plan

Step 4: Identify Target Markets

Step 5: Develop an Effective Sales Approach

Step 6: Needs Analysis

Step 7: Proposals and Presentations

Step 8: Negotiate

Step 9: Close

Step 10: Serve the Client

We find, however, that most practitioners spend little or no time in Steps 1 through 5—the most critical steps in the selling process to complete if Steps 6 through 10 are to result in a successful business transaction.

Each of the steps listed above is discussed in detail throughout this book. By focusing on achieving the goals, skills, and/or systems in each of these steps, you will lay the foundation for success in this highly competitive industry.

There are many factors that go into creating a successful broker. To begin with, it is critical that the practitioner has a clear understanding of the new sales model, and knows how to conduct the critical research necessary to develop a viable sales or leasing strategy. Other skills, such as knowing how to negotiate effectively, are useless, stand-alone skills in the context of an overall strategy for success.

The best place to begin developing the skills and *Systems for Success* you need is with a discussion of the traditional sales models vs. modern sales models.

The Traditional Sales Model

The traditional sales transaction could be described as a pyramid. At the top, you had a mere tip of what the traditional salesperson felt was important. At the bottom, you had the priority of where the salesperson put his or her effort. Segments of increasing size represent the relative emphasis the salesperson places on each successive phase of the sales call.

In the old sales model, the emphasis on "Knowledge and Information" represented about 10% of a successful sale. This included developing rapport with the tenant, establishing credibility, and creating common ground. In the traditional sales model, "Knowledge and Information" were at the tip of the sales pyramid, and the lowest of priorities for any salesperson.

Just below the tip of this traditional sales pyramid was "Needs Analysis." What does the tenant need? How can I provide him with it? How can I do this more efficiently? What are the unspoken needs? The *spoken* needs? How do they mesh? These all-important questions provided only 20% of the traditional sales call.

"The Presentation" came next, accounting for about 30% of the traditional sales call. This included the amount of information about the product or service that the salesperson provided to the tenant, as well as organization and delivery.

In the traditional sales model, the majority of the emphasis, in other words, the *bottom* of the pyramid, was on the "Summary and Close," which accounted for 40% of the salesperson's success.

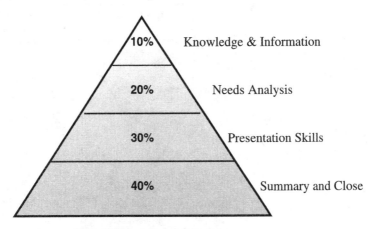

Traditional Sales Model

The New Sales Model

Today's competitive environment and modern view of selling challenges the traditional sales model, resulting in an "inverted pyramid." By turning the traditional sales model on its ear, this reduces the emphasis on "Summary and Close" and focuses on the importance of sound "Knowledge and Information," which establishes credibility, creates interest, and may account for 40% of all successful modern sales.

The critical need for thorough "Needs Analysis" now accounts for a full 30% of a successful sale, while "Presentation Skills" currently account for 20% of the sale. "The Close," traditionally considered the key phase, now only accounts for 10% of a successful sale.

How does that work? The successful broker knows that The Close, in many cases, is a mere formality when time has been spent building a good relationship with the prospect during the initial phase of the sales process. He succeeds in this vital and all-important area by demonstrating a thorough and exhaustive knowledge of the prospect's business and establishing interest in key solutions designed to address the prospect's identified vision, mission, or goals.

Top producers are no longer satisfied with the tradition sales call, resulting in only 100% effort. You shouldn't be, either . . .

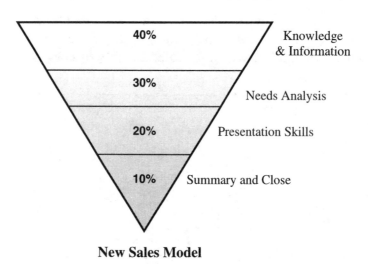

New Sales Model

You're Not Selling Real Estate; You're Selling Solutions

Top performers understand that commercial real estate, just like any other business, is not a static system in which one can rely on last year's models to provide this year's solutions. More than that, they understand the evolving role of their tenants, and keep up with what their tenants want—and how to give it to them.

Today's market-savvy and demanding tenants want long-term consultative relationships, not just one-time transactional deals. The majority of tenants need answers to their real estate problems and challenges that are entirely unrelated to relocation or other traditional real estate issues.

Successful brokers focus on the goals and practices of their tenants, and provide the type of quality service and support they now expect and demand. This is a result of **five key skills** for selling solutions: *researching* available options, *listening* to the tenant, *identifying* his needs, *offering* suitable options, and *providing* total solutions.

"People don't want to be *sold* anything. They want you to help them make *good buying decisions*."

—**Eileen Shay**

Today's commercial real estate environment is in constant demand for selected real estate services, which are rendered for a fee, with a consultative environment that is *relationship* driven rather than *transaction* driven. However, most brokers / salespeople do not think of themselves as "Service Providers." This is a critical mistake.

5 Suggestions for Selling Solutions

- **RESEARCH** available options
- **ASK** the right questions
- **LISTEN** to the tenant
- **IDENTIFY** their needs and opportunities
- **OFFER** total solutions designed to improve their business

Are You a Professional Real Estate Counselor?

The broker who continues to think and act like the "middleman," and not a "service provider," will eventually find himself left out of the equation altogether. The elimination of the middleman in our increasingly self-service economy—the travel agent, the investment broker, the middle manager—is a trend that will continue at an exponential rate, leaving those who aren't willing—or able—to adapt far, far behind.

The modern, agile, market-responsive broker is becoming *less* like a traveling salesman and *more* like a professional real estate counselor, a caring and compassionate practitioner who renders various real estate services on demand—and *for a fee*.

It is estimated that up to an additional 40% of total annual income could eventually come from non-transaction activities. The single most important resource you have to take advantage of this growing trend is "Knowledge and Information."

In today's speculative and competitive environment, many overeager and inexperienced brokers give away much—some would say *too* much—of their knowledge and information in anticipation of "getting a foot in the door."

Forget "On the Rim and Out the Door!" To capitalize on your newfound attitudes and selling strategies, so-called "Free" services must now be **un-bundled** and rendered, individually, for a fee. Much the same way an oil change is not included in a tune-up, or batteries don't come with your Walkman, your valuable services should no longer be provided "pro bono." What was once given away for "Free" to entice potential tenants is now called "Value Added Services" and *sold* to them.

Your expertise in the form of specialization should extend beyond property-type and territory, to tenant-type and category of services. Traditional transaction brokers specialize in terms of the type of property they deal with, and perhaps what type of transaction is contemplated as a result.

In your role as a "Professional Real Estate Counselor" as part of this new advisory environment, specialization will also include your entire *range of services*.

Providing Value-Added, Comprehensive Real Estate Services

The decisive benefit of establishing a full-service advisory relationship with your tenant is that you are building a solid foundation on which to grow. Traditional transaction-brokers overlook this trust-building stage—at their own peril—as they skip straight to the transaction level of the relationship in search of nothing short of "the deal."

As we discovered in the New Sales Model, this modern, consultative role of Professional Real Estate Counselor is revealed in the first phase, in which Knowledge and Information account for approximately 40% of the sale.

The payoff of developing this trust-building state with a tenant— with *all* your tenants—is that you will end up with more transactions as a result of your full-service approach to business. If your "sales" call is made, not with the intention of relocating your tenant, but to provide real estate information or a service, you will have a much greater chance of ending up with a transaction, as opposed to a rejection.

This is the strategy used by such successful firms and forward thinking organizations as Johnson Controls—they provide the service *with* the transaction. By practicing the same philosophy, you are now getting paid to develop the relationship, eliminating the "bake-off," and cutting out the competition.

Determining What Services to Offer

Half of the "value" of adding Value-Added, Comprehensive Services to your growing menu of business offerings is knowing exactly *what* to offer, or more specifically, *how much* of what to offer. Offering too much cuts into your profit, and offering too little could kill the sale.

You also don't want to begin delving into areas in which you don't specialize, such as distressed properties if your forte is commercial development. Spreading yourself too thin makes all of your Value-Added Services suffer, and not just the ones you have less experience providing.

To that end, begin providing your Comprehensive Services based upon your specialty. More importantly, brand *yourself* . . .

Branding *Yourself*

Ritz®. Coca-Cola®. Nike®. Equity Office®. General Growth®. These are brand names we all recognize, rely on, or feel comfortable using regularly. But brand names, or more importantly, the art of "branding," is not reserved for products and corporations alone.

You can brand—yourself. *You* become the broker to go to, each and every time, for *your* niche, specialty, or "brand." Begin to specialize by carefully selecting your range of services, and then getting to know— increasing your Knowledge & Information—each and every one until they become second nature.

Produce sales language—with support from promotional blurbs from friends and colleagues, professional awards and recognition, or even journal or magazine articles—positioning yourself as *the* expert on these services in the field.

Use your branding language in all of your marketing and promotional materials, such as brochures, flyers, and on your Website— and even your telephone answering service or what tenants hear while they're on hold. First, however, it is imperative that you determine your specialty or niche:

What is the focus of your practice?

- Industrial
- Retail
- Office

How are you recognized *within* **the specialty?**

- Service
- Financial
- Quick Sale
- Distressed Properties
- Class A Properties

3 Proven Steps to Making an Additional 40% Income!

Increasing your income by an extra 40% each year can be as simple—and profitable—as following these three proven steps:

1. Identify your firm's real estate strengths and assess their demand in the marketplace. Guesswork and luck aren't the way to earning more, precision and focus *are*. Vigorously research the current marketplace and compare it to your own personal strengths—and weaknesses—in the market. Then learn how to capitalize on those strengths—and avoid those weaknesses—to the best advantage by filling in the gaps.

2. Survey all your tenants, regardless of size, to determine their needs. Take the "guess"—and even some of the "work"—out of guesswork and answer your own questions by going straight to the source. Begin with an informal survey of your tenants.

For example: Mail out a simple survey form to each of your tenants, designed to determine their current and future needs, what services they lack, what services they currently utilize, whether they plan to expand or downsize in the future, what services they currently outsource, and so on.

Feedback from these surveys will identify areas of service, based on need, that you can offer *for a fee*, and will give you a clear indication of the types of services you should provide. If you *listen* to your tenants, they will *tell* you what they want.

3. Determine your flat hourly rate. To determine the "flat rate," estimate the approximate number of hours you will most likely require for the assignment and multiply that figure by your hourly rate. This will provide a no-nonsense estimate that shouldn't raise any eyebrows at the beginning of the relationship, or cause surprise when the services are provided.

33 Real Estate Services to Provide "for a Fee"

The following is a *partial* list of commercial real estate services to concentrate on, specialize in, brand yourself around and, most importantly, *provide for a fee*. While it is well worth reviewing to help develop your branding potential and decide which services to *suggest* offering, it is strongly recommended that the *tenant* be the one to dictate the type of services you provide:

- Service Contract Audit
- Strategic Distribution Overview (Map Service)
- Value Trends Analysis -- VTA (Property Analysis)
- Multiple Value Trends Analysis -- MVTA (Portfolio Analysis)
- Construction Management
- Annual Tax Incentive Survey/Locational Cost Analysis
- Lease Audit
- Labor Pool Analysis
- Due Diligence/Purchase Audit
- Early Lease Renewal
- Value/Risk Analysis
- Due Diligence Coordination & Review
- Contract Negotiation
- Property Valuations & Appraisals
- Land Development Scheduling
- Zoning/Subdivision Analysis
- Site Planning
- Signage Problems
- Space Planning
- Construction Documents

- Architectural & Engineering Interface
- Schematic Cost Estimate
- Preliminary Schedules
- Permits
- Punch List
- Pre-Construction Consultations
- Lease Administration
- Preventive Maintenance Programming
- Service Contract Specifications and Administration
- Lease Comparisons
- Capital Needs
- Tenant Representation
- Analysis of Relocation Cost

Getting Paid!

Providing new "services" that were once merely bundled together and given away for free will only provide additional income if you actually get *paid* for them. Having established these services, assembled targeted marketing material, identified your market niche, and branded yourself across all areas of your business, proper fee schedules should now be developed to assure that your services are, indeed, adequately paid for.

You should also consider researching, formatting, and rehearsing standardized presentations and template formats for each of these services, perfected over time, in order to provide them consistently, efficiently, and cost effectively.

Without suggesting a specific fee schedule for your particular services, the following chart is recommended for structuring fees for services based on the following concept:

<u>Hourly Rate Calculation</u>

Practitioner A wants to make $200,000 a year.

Practitioner A works 1,500 billable hours a year.

Suggested formula for determining "fee for service"

$200,000 x 2 = $400,000 (50% of the fee for the firm)

1500 hours   = $266.00 hourly rate

$266.00 x 1.40 (practitioner's overhead) = $372.40

$372.40 or $375 would be the flat hourly rate for fee service

---

Business Development and Marketing

5 Steps for Positioning the Property for Marketing

Positioning the property—identifying the best users—is the first step in the business development strategy, one that will enable you to market the property all the more effectively. Without effective positioning, all you are selling is square footage. (And tenants can buy that *anywhere*, from *anyone*.)

Marketing your property to the right user type is a more focused approach to business development, but it requires research and competitive analysis. First, study the features and benefits of your property, including tenant mix and other intangibles, such as architecture, technology, and location. Then, decide which of these specific attributes elevates the property value from that of your competition. Here is a brief discussion to guide your analysis:

1. Location. What is it about your building's location that sets it apart from the rest? Or that can be *used* to set it apart? Does it have the best access to the airport? Is it near the interstate for easier shipping, delivery, or commuting? Perhaps it is near the subway or bus line for employee convenience. Wherever you building may be, analyze it fully to paint the best picture possible about its location.

2. Services. These are perhaps the most flexible descriptors to promote. It's pretty hard to fudge about your building's location, and downright impossible to alter its *size*. But services are more self-reliant, more subjective, and thus can be tailored, modified, and improved upon to satisfy even the most reluctant customer. Perhaps you provide the best customer service, or at least the fastest response times. Also, you should list any value-added services provided, such as on-site conference facilities, cafeteria, or fine-dining restaurant; free laundry pick-up and delivery service; parking garage, on-site daycare, and so on. For services not readily available on site, a little research may reveal some nearby, readily accessible options worth mentioning.

3. Tenant Mix. What is it about the mix of current tenants that lends itself to prospective tenants? Is it a new business center, catering to technology that might attract cutting edge clientele? Does a majority of international trade mean a draw for the multicultural crowd? Does an overabundance of doctors' and lawyers' offices draw the same level of educated professionals? These are important questions to ask yourself as you look for the most sales potential from your tenant mix.

4. Building. First, consider the specific, physical features that set your actual building apart from the competition. For instance, is there something unique, perhaps even modern, about its architecture that you could use to your advantage? Is its size—big *or* small—a selling point? For instance, a large building may encourage sales language such as "comprehensive," "expansive," and "roomy." Yet a smaller building, otherwise viewed as a detriment, can be reinvented simply by using sales language such as "charming," "cozy," and "quaint." Be creative.

Perhaps it comes equipped with the latest technology, offering a satellite feed from rooftop access or twice the data ports of your competition. Whatever the present assets of your building, find some way to make them more attractive to potential tenants—and more profitable to you.

5. Position the Building. Use the information above to help position your building and identify your target market. **Some good examples:**

- Building "X" will be the choice of small to mid-sized business outsource service providers that want flexible space near the airport and convenience for hourly workers.

- Building "Y" will be the choice of high-end legal, accounting, and financial services companies that want first-rate service, prestige, and need to be near the federal courthouse.

Business Development Strategy

The Prospecting Pyramid

With the property correctly positioned, you can now begin to develop a strategy for marketing the property. Remember the four phases of the New Sales Model? They form the basis for the Business Development Strategy. Each phase of this strategy contributes its own, specific value to the success of the future sale.

The *Lipsey Prospecting Pyramid* is the system for implementing the Business Development Strategy.

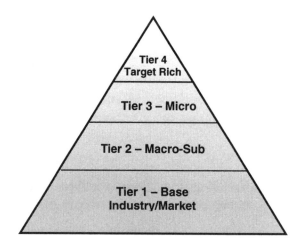

The following sections discuss the method and rationale behind the four levels that make up the development of the Prospecting Pyramid:

Tier 1 of the Prospecting Pyramid:

Identifying Your Target Industry/Market

Research provides the vital *Knowledge & Information* that is so necessary to help identify your target prospects with a view toward creating a focused and effective marketing campaign, customized, of course, for the type of product being marketed.

The basic research that forms the first level of the Prospecting Pyramid is based on the following qualifiers:

- **Economic Predictions** (local/national)

- **Industry** (absorption, occupancy, rent per sq. ft., gaps in market, etc.)

- **Trends** (service, design, promotion)

- **Growth Industries** (telecommunications, residential care facilities)

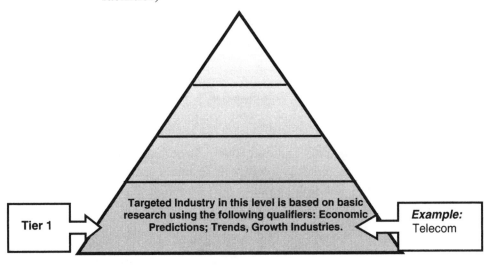

Tier 1

Targeted Industry in this level is based on basic research using the following qualifiers: Economic Predictions; Trends, Growth Industries.

Example: Telecom

Identifying which growing industry sector to target requires an understanding of the research necessary to project changes and trends on macro and micro economic levels. However, projecting economic, industry, and real estate trends are not straight-line calculations. So many factors are involved in these areas of research that even so-called techno-savvy computer models vary because of changes in assumptions made by economists and other "experts." Understanding macroeconomics will help use such trends to your advantage.

For example: If the economy is growing and interest rates are dropping, then overall demand for space will naturally be on the rise. If the unemployment rate is rising, the need for additional space is probably not as great.

The following is a targeted list of valuable sources and resources to be leveraged in developing the vital first tier (*Industry/Market*) of your Prospecting Pyramid:

- Local Newspapers
- *The Wall Street Journal*
- Business Publications
- Trade Publications
- Chambers of Commerce
- The Internet
- Economic Development Councils
- Economists

Who's Growing on a National Level?

When creating Tier 1 (*Researching Your Target Industry/Market*) economic predictions, think in terms of 1, 3, and 5 years. Use the following EXAMPLE charts to gather and assimilate the research and statistics you develop on your own:

Local Industry	Specific Companies	Comments/Projections

National Industry	Local Impact	Comments/Projections

Economic Factor	1 Year	3 Year	5 Year
Interest Rates (+/-) compared to today			
National Economic Growth (+/-) compared to today			
Local Economic Growth (+/-) compared to today			
Inflation (+/-) compared to today			

Trends in Design, Service, Customer Needs	1 Year	3 Year	5 Year
Lease Length			
Length of Time to Build-out			

Local Real Estate Factor	1 Year	3 Year	5 Year
Construction (+/-) Compared to Today			
Absorption (+/-) Compared to Today			
Changes in Local Factors (roads, airports, etc) (+/-) Compared to Today			
Occupancy (+/-) Compared to Today			

Finally, use the following chart to analyze research findings and to assist you in narrowing the focus and developing the second Tier (*Narrowing Your Focus*) of the Prospecting Pyramid:

Industry	Will I target them?	What will space needs be?	What other services?
Health Care			
Education			
Hotels			
Computer Science			
Finance			
Bio & Medial			

10 Methods to Track Commercial Real Estate Market Trends

- Spend at least three hours a week reading magazines and journals that report general market trends.

- Read trade magazines specific to your industry.

- Subscribe to Internet services that feed market information to your computer.

- Subscribe to newsletters in your field.

- Use Infotrac—a computerized database for researching business, management, finance, trade, and investment topics.

- Set up a monthly "Trend Watch" lunch with colleagues.

- Attend meetings of your local trade association.

- Subscribe to services that provide industry- or market-specific polling data.

- Talk with salespeople outside your industry.

- Talk with your customers.

Tier 2 of the Prospecting Pyramid:

Narrowing Your Focus

Use the numbers and information gathered in the preceding charts and research methods to examine the trends within each industry and narrow your focus for the development of the second level of the Prospecting Pyramid: *Narrowing Your Focus.*

Always use a second qualifier to concentrate on a specialized segment of the market within the chosen industry, such as "Long Distance," which is a more focused category in the overall field of "Telecommunications;" or use financial drivers, such as those companies within the specific industry who fall within a certain attractive percentage of growth.

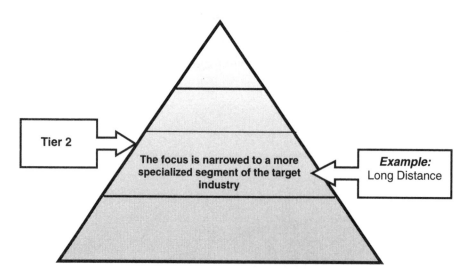

Tier 3 of the Prospecting Pyramid:
Zooming In

The next two all-important phases of the Prospecting Pyramid—*Zooming In* and *Selecting Your Target*—are fine-tuned, specific, and narrowly focused. It is at these two critical levels that all sales and marketing efforts build directly toward the sale and during which time most of the one-on-one, personalized sales effort is concentrated to maximum effect.

Specifically for this third tier, *Zooming In*, you should begin concentrating your efforts on targeted strategies to fine-tune your priorities toward the specific market you are aiming for. In our continuing sample pyramid, for example, by now you have narrowed your target down from the broader base of *Telecommunications* to the smaller field of *Long Distance*.

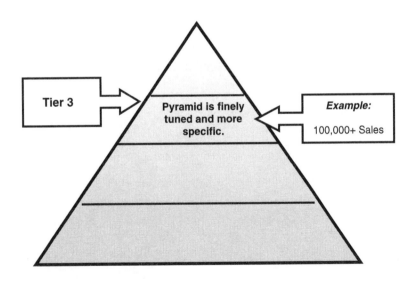

As you "zoom in" even closer on your target market, you should further fine tune this decision and make it even more specific, such as "what size of user am I looking for in this broad field of

Telecommunications, and the even narrower, more focused field of Long Distance?"

A good answer might be some specific sales goal, such as, targeting companies with 100,000+ sales in the Long Distance market. Now you are honing in on a specific size or economically viable user. The result is a highly qualified target market on which you can focus all sales efforts.

Tier 4 of the Prospecting Pyramid:

Selecting Your Target

In the fourth and final phase of the Prospecting Pyramid—*Selecting Your Target*—you are finally ready to determine the end-result of all this research and information. You've narrowed the field down from *Telecommunications* to *Long Distance*, and even further selected a realistic, specific goal, such as *100,000+ sales in the targeted field of Long Distance*.

Now it is time to decide *where* to best take advantage of this specific market. In our example, we'll use Dallas, where the goal of reaching 100,000+ sales in the growing field of Long Distance, which branches out from the overall field of Telecommunications, is entirely reachable.

Focused market research and proper analysis of growth trends will be your two most valuable assets in zeroing in on this last, specific target.

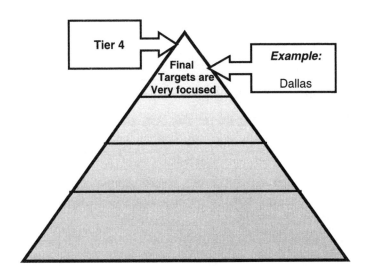

Michael J. Lipsey

How to Develop a Measurable Sales/Leasing Plan

One of the most critical components of any successful sales or leasing plan is the development of a systematic, measurable approach to achieving the goal.

Without a quantifiable plan, the ability to achieve set financial, sales, or leasing goals become "hit or miss." Our systematic approach to achieving sales or leasing goals will not only ensure that you attain those goals, but they provide the client, owner, or manager with a measurable system for tracking sales and leasing activity on a daily, weekly or monthly basis.

We will assume that the following benchmarks need to occur to result in a single signed lease:

1. Lease Signed
2. Negotiation
3. Letters of Intent
4. Proposals
5. Showings
6. Contacts
7. Daily Units

A Unit is any activity that generates interest in the property.

A Contact is any person-to-person contact/discussion related to the property.

We will also make the following assumptions regarding the ratios between the various benchmarks. We will assume the following for a two-year leasing plan:

32   Tenants will require

64   Lease negotiations

128   Letter of Intent

384   Proposals

1,536   Site Visits

7,680   Contacts

76,800 Units of Activity

Spread over a two-year timeframe, we arrive at the following Sales Plan (shown is Year 1 only)

ACTIVITY	Month 1	Month 2	Month 3	Month 4	Month 5	Month 6
Units of Activity	3,200	3,200	3,200	3,200	3,200	3,200
Contacts	320	320	320	320	320	320
Visits	64	64	64	64	64	64
Proposals	16	16	16	16	16	16
Letters of Intent	6	6	6	6	6	6
Lease Negotiation	2	2	2	2	2	3
Signed Leases		1	1	1	2	2
Cumulative Tenants		1	2	3	5	7

ACTIVITY	Month 7	Month 8	Month 9	Month 10	Month 11	Month 12
Units of Activity	3,200	3,200	3,200	3,200	3,200	3,200
Contacts	320	320	320	320	320	320
Visits	64	64	64	64	64	64
Proposals	16	16	16	16	16	16
Letters of Intent	6	6	5	5	5	5
Lease Negotiation	3	3	3	3	3	3
Signed Leases	1	1	1	2	1	2
Cumulative Tenants	8	9	10	12	13	15

If the plan is managed on a monthly basis and all benchmarks are met, then at the end of Year 2, the Cumulative Tenants will be 32, as expected. The key benefit of developing a sales/leasing matrix is that it allows the practitioner, manager, owner, or client to gauge whether the plan is on track and make adjustments as needed in order to remain on target.

The examples above track every measurable aspect and activity involved in the sale or leasing process. Should you wish to develop a less detailed sales/leasing matrix, we propose the Short Form Sales/Leasing Plan, which still provides measurable benchmarks designed to keep the sales/leasing goals on track.

	Month 1	Month 2	Month 3	Month 4	Month 5	Month 6
Meetings						
Proposals						
Contracts						
Closed Transactions						

11 Benefits of a Sizzling Sales/Leasing Plan

- Sets measurable, specific, vivid, and motivating goals
- Identifies the benchmarks necessary to achieve ultimate goals
- Outlines a logical order among the intermediate steps
- Establishes a reasonable yet challenging timeline
- Pinpoints the barriers between you and your objectives
- Specifies strategies, procedures, and tactics
- Summarizes the resources needed
- Establishes accountability
- Is in writing
- Signifies commitment
- Will win assignments

Avoiding the Sales Cliff

Before embarking on any business development strategy, especially an exciting new one such as this, remember the "Sales Cliff." More importantly, remember to *avoid its trappings*. In the Sales Cliff analogy, the typical salesperson focuses most of his energy and much of his time on the exciting and energizing transaction at hand.

In doing so, however, he ends up almost completely ignoring Tiers 1 and 2 of the Prospecting Pyramid, thereby setting himself up for an empty prospecting "pipeline" when the current transaction is complete.

In order to avoid falling off the Sales Cliff, one must always keep the prospect pipeline full. For instance, most busy brokers do not spend much time (or *any* time at all when they are very busy) working the lower two tiers of the prospecting pyramid. Unfortunately, as we now know, these are precisely the two levels that target the highest volume of prospects.

If no time is spent keeping the prospecting pipeline full (for instance, by keeping the broadcast e-mails and bulk mailers flowing to potential new tenants) then when the sales crunch is over and the deals are done, the broker can now turn his attention to the next prospect. However, there *is* no next prospect because he has not been working (or has not had someone else working) the pipeline.

As a result, he falls off the prospecting sales cliff and has to claw his way up from the bottom all over again. Keeping the prospecting pipeline full establishes him as "king of the hill" at all times and allows him to focus his attention and valuable time on the top two tiers of the target market.

Effective Marketing Strategies

In this phase of the *Systems for Success* Selling Program, you begin to market to the four tiers of the Prospecting Pyramid using various marketing strategies. The goal is to keep the pipeline full while at the same time working the top two target-rich tiers with a more focused, personal marketing campaign. In other words, the strategy is to focus your energies and utilize resources in a way that will allow you to leverage and integrate all of your efforts that build toward the sale.

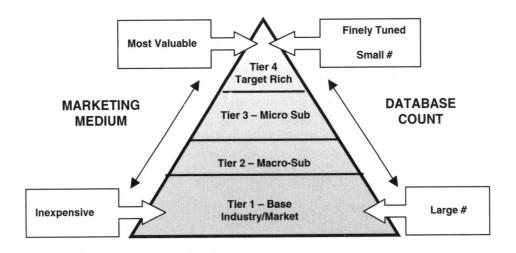

At Tiers 1 and 2, the marketing campaign should be cost effective, automated, and delegated in order to capitalize on your time. Prospects in the first two tiers should receive broadcast emails or faxes, bulk mailers, and general flyers. With thousands of potential prospects in these two categories, this is simply the most effective way to market.

At levels three and four, the broker's marketing efforts should be more personal and professional. Four-color package mailings and personalized letters are appropriate first steps in Tier 3. Personal calls and meetings with the decision-maker are appropriate for Tier 4. It is at this level that the broker must demonstrate his *Knowledge and Information* of the target prospect, and maybe even propose viable business solutions to identified industry/company issues, if he is going to succeed in creating interest in the initial stages of the sale.

15 Marketing Mediums That *Work*

Marketing is an art form that many seek, but few master. Begin creating your own version of Marketing Mastery with the following 15 Marketing Mediums That *Work*:

- Tenant Referrals
- Public Relations
- Newsletters
- Direct Mail—Make it Memorable!
- Listings on the Internet—Search Engines, Links, Etc.
- Share information among divisions to support Cross Selling
- Sponsorship
- Shared Database
- Community Involvement
- Public Speaking
- Referral Organizations
- Trade shows
- Email
- Faxing
- Advertising

12 Opportunities for Prospecting in Commercial Real Estate

After applying the latest numbers, using the recent trends, and analyzing various economic factors, the following are thirteen other avenues of opportunity that currently exist to make you a Top Performer:

- Management deficiencies
- Competitor's tenants receiving poor service
- Buildings with vacant space that have cut back on services
- Operating deficits
- Lack of capital improvements
- Owners who need liquidity
- Interior or exterior deterioration
- Functional obsolescence
- Frontage changes
- Traffic congestion
- Access changes
- Buildings that are completely full (tenants may need more space and can't get it)

9 Assets You Already Have

If you are searching for new prospects, don't forget about the ones you already have! You probably have hundreds of potential prospects you are not paying attention to because they are right under your very nose: your present customers. Consider these nine assets already stacked in your favor:

- They know you
- You have established a rapport
- Confidence and trust have been built
- You have a history of delivery and satisfaction
- They respect you
- They use (and like) your product or service
- They will return your call
- They will be more receptive to your presentation and product offering
- They have credit and have paid you in the past

6 Ways to ID Commercial Real Estate Customers

Identifying customers is an often challenging—and occasionally elusive—practice that sets the Top Performer apart from the typical broker or agent. Below are six specific tactics Top Performers use to identify potential—or perhaps even current—customers.

- Write an article about your specialty and submit it to a newsletter that is subscribed to by your prospective target market.

- Accept or seek an opportunity to speak at a function.

- Establish a lasting relationship with a tenant by periodically asking about his business, and not always looking for the quick sale and moving on to the next transaction.

- Make a cold call if you are in the area and have time before your next appointment.

- Hold a seminar on hot issues and invite potential customers. Don't hard sell them; give them knowledge about your specialty/new issues and how it will impact their business.

- Do volunteer work in the community.

Referrals are Like Gold:
Treat Them That Way!

Sales referrals are a lucrative and elusive stream of profit-generating revenue—if you know how to court them. Many inexperienced brokers treat such referrals as "sure things," and rush them too soon with inefficient sales practices. But Top Performers know that sales referrals are like gold—and they treat them that way.

Below is a list of ten proven rules for treating your next sales referral like the prize he or she really is:

10 Rules to Ensure Success with a Referral

- Approach with care, be prepared, and don't move too quickly.
- Arrange a three-way meeting (social event, lunch, networking event).
- Get personal information about the referral before you make the first contact.
- You don't have to sell at the first meeting if your customer is with you.
- Arrange a second, private meeting to get down to business.
- Try to get the prospect to prepare information for your meeting.
- Don't send too much information in the mail, just enough to create interest.
- Write a personal note to the referral within 24 hours. Be brief and positive.
- Write your customer a thank you note for the referral; include a gift.
- Deliver!

The Phone Line is Your *Best* Tool . . .

Old-fashioned brokers, unlike successful salespeople, see the phone line as one simple tool in an already limited arsenal of sales weaponry.

Today's savvy broker knows that the phone line provides much more than a simple voice connection. It's an effective tool with a variety of other uses—Email, Internet, voice mail, and fax—to assure maximum exposure for this underrated—and invaluable—sales tool.

The following is a vital list of *5 Ways to Use Your Phone Line as a Marketing Tool*. Each will be explained more fully in the following pages:

- **Voice** – *Phone*
- **Broadcast** – *Fax*
- **Information** – *Email*
- **Research** – *Internet*
- **Contact** – *Voice Mail*

12 Tips for Cold Calling Success

As we have seen, the telephone can be a valuable sales tool. From fax machines to Email providers, that fiber-optic line to the outside world can mean money and profit for those Top Performers who know how to utilize it efficiently. And no task is more rewarding—or daunting—than the telephone cold call.

While countless books have been written on this very topic, here are 11 simple tips to help you when you need it the most—right here, right now:

- **Have a specific objective for the call before you pick up the phone.** Every phone call is an opportunity, but it can be a wasted one if you're simply making an off-the-cuff stab.

- **Know the purpose of your call.** Why are you calling? Why should your tenant buy? How can you help them? How do they want to be helped? These are all questions to ask yourself before picking up the phone.

- **Relay the purpose of your call and ask for the appropriate contact.** Don't waste time with the shipping department if the person you *really* need is in receiving, and vice versa.

- **Transfer quickly.** After finding out the name of the decision maker, ask to be transferred to him or her.

- **Ask permission.** Ask the decision-maker if you can assist in the improvement of their ability to conduct business using your service.

- **Anticipate Objections**. Be prepared with a collection of well-thought-out responses to common objections.

- **Write Responses from the Prospect's Perspective**. Ask yourself, "If *I* were the prospect, what issues, thoughts, and words would make *me* want to book an appointment?"

- **Speak Deliberately**. Talking at a consistent pace conveys a message of confidence and control. A great tip is to play your responses into your voice mail, then listen to make sure you sound convincing.

- **Sound Passionate About What You Are Saying**. Focus on the value you bring to the table. When you believe in what you say, others will believe in you.

- **Fine-tune Your Responses**. Ask yourself what didn't work after each call. Every conversation is a valuable resource.

- **Use Objections to Influence Fence Sitters**. If someone is uncommitted, mention the objection you think is behind the indecision. This enables you to take command and respond passionately.

- **Make the Call**

(**Source**: *Stoddart Publishing*)

10 Voice Mail Tips

Leaving an effective voice mail is half the battle, once you've made it past the receptionist-slash-gatekeeper. Many salespeople negatively view getting a prospect's voice mail as a sign of defeat: "Oh no, another missed opportunity!" But Top Performers view the prospect of leaving an engaging, inviting, and informative voice mail as a golden opportunity. Now, completely uninterrupted, you have a marvelous chance to get your sales message across in the most efficient, appropriate, and controlled manner possible. But only if the opportunity is ripe:

- **Speak slowly**. There's nothing worse than a rushed message. Not only will you sound nervous and amateurish—but desperate. As well, half your message will get lost in the translation.

- **Leave your phone number twice**. The recipient shouldn't have to replay your message over and over simply to get your contact information.

- **Spell your name**. It's a simple—but worthwhile—step to making sure the recipient gets it right the first time.

- **Don't just leave information, leave a** *message*. Prepare something before leaving the message, a possible solution for an industry challenge

- **Make it quick**. Longer than 60 seconds, and you risk losing your audience.

- **Give your message a headline**. This helps the recipient distinguish which calls are a top priority.

- **Enunciate clearly**. The audio quality of voice mail varies dramatically. Speak up and state your business clearly.

- **Be specific about what you want**. Leave a numbered list or steps for the tenant to mark off.

- **Avoid "thank-you" messages**. These are never welcome, as they only add to the daily voice mail overload most tenants must contend with.

- **Don't leave repeat messages**. Your second call is no more likely to be returned than your first. Try sending an Email instead.

Here are a few thoughts on when to leave a message, and when *not* to leave a message:

When TO Leave a Message:

- When you have spoken with the prospect before and received positive feedback.

- When you are following up on an interested lead.

- When you have valuable information the prospect really needs to know about.

- When you have prepared a message that has enough impact to get the prospect to respond.

(Adapted from *The Sales Bible* by Jeffrey H. Gitomer)

12 Tips for Incoming Phone Calls

There are enough gatekeepers out there, don't *be* one! Top Performers test their own phone systems as often as they navigate those of others. Why not do the same by implementing these seven great tips for incoming phone calls to your office:

- **Call your company and ask for yourself**. This is a great way to see how effective—or confusing—your existing phone system might be. Call yourself before work to see if anyone picks up, if your voice mail gets routed directly, or if it simply rings. If something irks you, think how badly it would irk a potential customer.

- **Call your company as if you were a potential or active customer**. Ask for information, ask for different departments, voice a complaint, leave a message asking for a callback, etc., all the reasons people call. Do it a few times a week to see if the system if up to snuff. If not, change it.

- **The 2-Ring Policy**. Institute a policy in which everyone in your office answers the phone in two rings—or less. When it's answered, say something meaningful and pleasant. Say it slowly so the caller can understand you. Do it every time the phone rings.

- **Take messages completely and accurately**. Develop a system that works for you, be it on your computer, in a notepad, on the backs of business cards, etc. Always repeat vital information back to the caller before he or she hangs up.

- **Listen to your menu options**. Play devil's advocate and see if your menu options are confusing, meandering, our outdated. Keep what works, throw out the rest, and start over if you have to. Do this until your system is flawless.

- **Don't use a speaker phone.** Unless, of course, it is a conference call and the tenant has requested it or understands why it is being used. Speaker phones give the impression that you are doing something other than concentrating on the call.

- **Ask before you put someone on hold.** While they are on hold, get back to them within 60 seconds. Also, instead of using music in the background, consider recording a professional commercial or reading from your sales literature.

- **When you answer the phone, be warm and enthusiastic**. Your voice at the end of the telephone line is sometimes the only impression of your company a caller will get.

- **Identify yourself and your organization**. For instance, you might say, "Good morning, Prime Properties. Malcolm speaking. How may I help you?" No one should ever have to ask if they've reached your business.

- **Control your language**. Don't use slang or jargon. Instead of saying, "Sure," "Maybe," or "Okay," say "Certainly," "Of course," "Very well," or "All right."

- **Be up, even when you're "down**." For example, rather than saying, "I don't know," say, "Let me find out about that for you."

- **Return all calls within one business day**. This isn't just common courtesy; it's just plain common "sense."

4 Ways to Utilize Your Fax

While email has, in many ways, replaced broadcast faxing as a medium for marketing, broadcast faxing is still a viable, convenient, and inexpensive tool that should be leveraged. Remember the following guidelines:

- The fax continues to get immediate attention. You have a page or two to get information to your prospect—use the space wisely. Say only what is necessary to achieve your next objective.

- Creativity is essential. If your fax is clever, different, and contains concise information, you will gain confidence and attention from its reader(s).

- Always fax on the fine or detail setting. It takes longer, but when your fax comes through crisp and clear to your prospect, it reflects the quality of your company—and vice versa.

- Watch the graphics and pictures. You have most likely received a fax that contains text and then a black box—which may at one time or another have resembled a picture or graphic. If you don't have to include it, get rid of it. It only takes more time to print and doesn't look professional unless done right.

8 Fax Broadcast Tips

Whether you are utilizing ACT! or a similar contact management system, to get the most from that vital office phone line, you should be maximizing the software in your possession by sending broadcast faxes on a regular basis. With many such systems, you can actually fax to your contact records without having to print information first. Remember the following guidelines:

- **Use targeted lists**. Nothing turns off a prospect like receiving an irrelevant fax.

- **Remove redundant numbers**. The only thing that turns off a prospect more than one irrelevant fax—is several of them!

- **Sort your list by first name**. If you sort by company or fax number and you want to send to multiple people at the same number, you get more busy signals and your fax job will take longer to complete.

- **Use the latest fax software**. If you have any kind of fax software, use it. If you don't, *get* it.

- **Fax yourself first**. This assures that both your images and copy look exactly like you want them to, *before* you send them out.

- **Send in "fine" mode**. Even if you want your fax to go out in standard mode, faxes will be much cleaner in this format.

- **Send "information" after hours**. Service reports, newsletters, and the like can be sent at any time and still get read. Normally, after 8 p.m. is best so that it can be sorted with the rest of the mail in the morning.

- **Promote yourself before lunch**. Promotional materials should go out between 10 a.m. and 1 p.m., if possible, in order to "catch" the reader during the day.

Email Gets it There!

Email is fast, cheap, and reliable! It's the best way to get information to your prospects in a timely and efficient manner. If you are using a contact management system, it should support broadcast Emailing as well. Unlike faxing, the quality of your documents and photographs will be maintained across most software platforms, assuring uniform delivery of your message.

A Commercial Real Estate Email Success Story

According to Dean L. Curci, "As a result of marketing four of Cap Rate Properties listings through a combination of targeted mass Emailings and advertisement at our web site, we were able to find the right buyer suited for each of the deals..." (Cap Rate Properties is based in Newport Beach, and the properties were leased to PayLess Drug, Circuit City, Albertson's, and Blockbuster Music.)

---

5 Rules of Email Etiquette

Despite its ease—or perhaps *because* of it—many people forget simple business etiquette when using this convenient and inexpensive system. Remember the following guidelines to avoid falling into this trap:

- Messages should be concise and to the point. Always think of an Email as a telephone conversation, except that you are typing instead of speaking.

- Don't get caught up in grammar and punctuation, especially *excessive* punctuation.

- Keep the number of characters per line below the 80-character limit.

- If you normally address a person as Miss/Mrs./Ms./Mr. Smith, then that is the way you should initially address them in an Email. If you normally call them by their first name, then you should either omit the salutation or follow the guideline specified in the prior sentence.

- It is recommended that you only use abbreviations that are already common to the English language, such as FYI and ASAP. Beyond that, you run the risk of confusing your recipient.

4 Email Don'ts

- ***Don't*** send an Email written entirely in UPPERCASE letters. Use of uppercase words is the equivalent of shouting in someone's ear! ONLY use uppercase words when trying to make a point that you feel strongly about, such as timely information or words that would otherwise be in bold or italics. Even at that, you should be careful with who you are exchanging messages. For instance, an Email to an executive or CEO will rarely sound as casual as one to a fellow broker or a secretary.

- ***Don't*** make a comment about grammar or punctuation in a reply to an incoming Email. Nobody wants to feel like they are exchanging Emails with their eighth-grade English teacher, and no one ever made a collateral sale by correcting someone.

- ***Don't*** send repeat Email information without getting permission to do so and/or allowing the recipient to inform you that they would like to be removed from the Email list.

- ***Don't*** forget to run your spell checker! (Every time you send an Email!)

Email Signature Line: *Your Virtual Business Card*

An extremely effective marketing tool that could potentially accompany each and every one of your daily Emails is known as an Email "signature line." Found at the bottom of an Email message, the signature line takes the place of a sender's "signature" in a regular letter.

But more than that, a well-crafted, targeted signature line can become a sender's virtual business card by listing vital, Internet-related information readers can easily "click" on, such as Website URLs, Email addresses, special offers, Ezines, newsletters, listing information, etc.

Anything you want a current or prospective tenant to know about can be placed in a succinctly written, massively targeted signature line attached to each and every one of your outgoing Emails. Just make sure to keep the total number of lines for the signature down to four or less, as in the example below:

SAMPLE SIGNATURE LINE:

Michael J. Lipsey, Author

SYSTEMS FOR SUCCESS*: The Ultimate Guide to Selling, Leasing, Presenting, Negotiating & Serving in Real Estate*

Email: mike@lipseyco.com

Website: www.lipseyco.com/success-systems

The Internet: *Use It to Increase Sales & Leasing Activity*

The most accessible—and widely used—form of marketing today is the Internet. From Websites to Email, this vital tool is often under-appreciated—and under-utilized—by countless brokers, yet capitalized upon by *every* Top Performer in commercial real estate today.

What can you gain from the Internet? A better question might be, what *can't* you gain? From up-to-the-minute commercial real estate listings to tracking industry trends with lightning speed, today's best Websites provide valuable information for the price of your local Internet or cable provider.

Where should you start? *Systems for Success* suggests beginning your tour of the World Wide Web exactly where your online customers will—by building your very own Website.

6 Reasons Why *You* Should Have a Corporate Website

A corporate Website may not double your company's revenues overnight, but it certainly offers plenty of other benefits that, in the long run, will lower sales costs and boost profits. A corporate Website:

- **Builds Customer Loyalty:** A well designed and easy to navigate Website should offer concise, detailed information about the organization, its people, products, and services.

- **Speeds the Sales Process:** Electronic sites offer the convenience, simplicity, and immediacy that sophisticated customers demand.

- **Improves Relationships:** Successful commercial sites anticipate, and answer, routine customer problems—allowing salespeople to concentrate on the strategic issues that forge strong vendor/customer ties.

- **Lower Marketing Costs:** Well-designed Websites include a comprehensive marketing campaign by providing a complete listing of available space and/or product with links that provide detailed information and visuals for each property you are marketing. This is, by far, your most cost-effective marketing tool. Be sure that your CD Business Card has a link to this site.

- **Collects Data:** Use your Website's tools to collect data on your visitors, whether by letting them sign a guest book, soliciting their Email addresses through an online newsletter, or checking your site statistics.

- **Provide Positive PR:** Post your latest press release online to allow savvy modern editors instant access to your latest news, deals, and announcements!

Leveraging the Power of the Internet

Today, a technology-enabled sales force is no longer a competitive advantage: It is a competitive *necessity*. Working smarter and faster will be the key for the success of the commercial real estate practitioner. Furthermore, it is the inevitable strategy—and daily practice—of the thriving Top Performer.

The Top Performer understands that while he may or may not have been born with a natural gift for technology, he must nonetheless capitalize on every advantage available to him.

Without capitalizing on the lightning speed of modern technology, you will slowly, but inevitably, fail. Technology allows us to do things quicker, faster, smarter, swifter, easier, and better.

Despite the difficulty synonymous with mastering technology, using technology doesn't mean you have to become a computer guru; you simply have to incorporate the technology tools currently—and widely— available to you and maximize their potential.

A Commercial Real Estate Internet Success Story

Clair Hotten, of Hotten Investment Real Estate in Walnut Creek, California, recently placed an apartment complex for sale online at $1,200,000. Within 15 minutes of posting the property, a prospective buyer from Fremont, CA called after having seen the online listing. The buyer immediately set up an appointment to see the property and wrote an offer to purchase that same day. The offer was accepted the next day and recently closed escrow.

---

12 Tips for Selling on the Internet

- Set specific, strategic goals for the site
- Contract the services of a professional Website developer
- Contact the services of a professional ISP (Internet Service Provider)
- Put your Web address in directories
- Link your site with search engines
- Connect hot links to your site
- Design an interactive site and make it very easy to use
- Make it appealing
- Make sure it is secure and protected
- Make sure all your copy is accurate and grammatically correct
- Monitor its use and its effect
- Constantly update the site

5 Things Commercial Real Estate Advertising Can Do for You

There is no better way to increase your status as a Top Performer than with a targeted, sensible, reasonable, appropriate, and well-planned *advertising campaign*. Advertising allows you to spread your message in a way word-of-mouth simply can't, but shouldn't replace good sales practices, reliable customer service, and delivering on your promise as a branded broker.

Here are five things advertising can do for you:

1. Create brand awareness
2. Generate inquiries
3. Promote special offers
4. Generate repeat business
5. Create BUZZ

7 Tips for Getting the Biggest Bang for your Advertising Buck

The myth that the biggest advertising budget is the *best* advertising budget is just that: a myth. Throwing money away on billboard ads in underdeveloped areas, radio time when none of your potential tenants are listening, and magazine ads in periodicals they don't read is a waste of time—and money!

As with everything else in life, there are a few secrets to getting the most out of your advertising budget, no matter how big—or small—it may be. Here are just a few:

- Set measurable objectives: Compare the number of incoming calls/visits/ proposals/negotiations/sales that you will get as a result of advertising vs. not advertising at all. Then spend accordingly.

- Pinpoint the medium you wish to advertise in: radio, flyers, postcards, Website banner ads, industry publications, etc.

- Hire an advertising firm or freelancer to do the work for you so that current/future projects aren't affected by reduced manpower.

- Look at the work your chosen advertising firm has done for other tenants of similar size—and with similar budgets—to better gauge the services you require.

- Don't ask for finished art or ideas as part of a presentation, unless you are prepared to give each presenter a fee.

- Ask who will handle your account (the owner will probably not do the day-to-day work).

- Be sure to preview layout proofs, artwork, color schemes, etc., along the way.

Advertising Pay-out Analysis Checklist

Advertising is only a smart—and effective—move when there is a profitable pay-out. Like any other aspect of commercial real estate, effective research and proper planning are essential elements to making your advertising dollar stretch for you. To help you analyze a potential pay-out from any future advertising campaigns, here is a list of potential items to first consider:

- **Measurable Objectives**: Will there be an actual increase in sales, inquiries, and profits as a result of the advertising?

- **Comparison/Base period without promotion**: Will the sales, inquiries, and profits remain the same?

- **Cost**: How much will the advertising cost?

- **Gross Results**: The actual number of sales, inquiries, and profits that result from your advertising campaign.

- **Net Results**: The difference between gross results and base period.

- **Effectiveness**: Compare the dollars spent with the business actually generated, then revisit your model to adjust advertising mediums and costs accordingly.

30 Advertising Tips

- Keep ad copy as simple as possible. Generally, less copy and more white space will grab the viewer's attention.

- If you're thinking about advertising online with a banner ad, remember the Internet is a powerful global medium—but not a proven medium for local advertising.

- Consider your target market. Will your customers see and respond to the ad you're about to place on television?

- If your budget allows, pay a professional to record your radio spots. Although most stations will produce the spot for free (in exchange for advertising on their station), the quality is often low and the voice too familiar.

- Effective advertising stems from a sound marketing plan.

- Advertising agencies offer excellent support to a long-term marketing plan. You might benefit from hiring an agency, even for a year, to get a strong grasp of your advertising direction.

- Your advertising rate will decrease by signing a longer-term contract.

- The moment you get tired of hearing or seeing your ads is usually the moment your audience begins to respond. Continue running them for another six months.

- The best ideas in advertising are often the *simplest* ideas.

- Ask yourself: "Is my message clear at a glance? Can the audience tell what the advertisement is about?"

- Develop headlines that entertain and communicate benefits to the reader.

- Repeat your message. Repeat your message. Repeat your message .

- Have a toll-free number and heavily promote it. A prospect is more likely to call if it's on your dime.

- Try running two quarter page ads in the same publication instead of one half-page ad.

- Your message on a billboard *must* be absorbed in three seconds or less.

- Use small brochures and postcards about your company to hand out, have available in your lobby, or mail to prospects.

- Word-of-mouth advertising cannot be bought. It is earned. And it's the best.

- Once a year buy something useful with your company name, logo, and phone number on it to give out. Overall, the cost is low for the exposure and pass-along rate of these specialty items.

- Write an article about your profession and submit it to the local press. Once published, you will be perceived as an expert in the field.

- Special interest supplements in local newspapers are usually read by fewer people, but the audience is more targeted.

- Consider a larger number of smaller ads instead of sinking your budget into one full-page ad. The consistent message and constant contact will get a higher response over time.

- Some newspapers and magazines find themselves needing to fill ad space at the eleventh hour. These ads are more affordable and sometimes larger than you might normally expect. Ask about these opportunities

- Inspiration for good advertising comes from many sources. When you see something that inspires you, clip it and save it.

- Make your advertising reflect your corporate culture and personality. Express yourself.

- Use action words in your body copy. Certain words will help "drive" the reader through the ad toward the message and benefit.

- Some online advertising can be had for free by using link exchanges and partnerships with sites of similar interests. Negotiate online deals with successful Websites to drive traffic to your site. It might take a while to establish these relationships but it will be worth it.

- Message strength is more important than the location and rotation of the ads.

- Good advertising pays for itself. Bad advertising is an expense.

- Watch what your competition is doing and where they're advertising.

- Give your advertising time to work.

Michael J. Lipsey

12 Rules for a Direct Mail Campaign

One of the most tried and tested avenues of profitable advertising revenue is a direct mail campaign. Yet like all facets of advertising, a profitable direct mail campaign is only as good as the strategy behind it. Printing, packing, and postage costs make direct mailings an efficient, if not FREE, venture. To make sure your direct mail campaign actually works, here are *12 Rules for Direct Mail*:

- **Develop something unique**. Create a message that will be remembered—and an item that will be kept.

- **Keep it inexpensive**. All marketing efforts need to pay-out. Direct mail is no exception.

- **Use First Class Mail**. When you care enough to send the very best…

- **Don't send more than 25-35 per week**. Sending more makes it hard to follow up.

- **Call 5-7 days after the mailing**. Your mailing now gives you an opening.

- **Verify receipt of the piece**. Confirm that the intended recipient has the piece you are referring to.

- **Begin with an "IBS," Introductory Benefit Statement**. This should create immediate interest or at least willingness to listen.

- **Determine current needs**. Use CENULARR (See pages 92 – 93 of *SYS*.)

- **Set an appointment**. After all, this is the *real* motivation behind any mailing.

- **Call back in 90 days**. Follow up at a later date if no immediate interest is expressed.

- **Send a second mailing in six months**. Cement your relationship with more information that is specific for what you now know about the tenant.

- **Follow-up**. And begin the process all over again.

14 Tips for Getting Your Direct Mail Read

- Use plain envelopes without windows.
- Don't fill the envelope with inserts.
- Address the envelope to a specific person, not "Occupant."
- Use white or conservatively colored paper.
- Use a readable font.
- Through variation in fonts, underling, bold, and italics, draw attention to important phrases and words.
- Experiment with unusual letter layouts and formats.
- Be sure to grab your reader's attention at the beginning of the letter.
- Keep the text simple.
- Write with an informal, flowing style.
- Don't end the first page with a period.
- Call for action.
- Sign your name in blue ink.
- Add a postscript that poses an intriguing question.

Networking in the Commercial Real Estate Industry

Networking is the very business of creating referrals. However, networking can be time consuming—it requires that you spend some time selling other people's services—and it requires that you are selective about who you network *with*.

Networking begins by looking at those with whom you already do business, such as:

- Accountants
- Lawyers
- Contractors
- Surveyors
- Environmental Engineers
- Retail Managers
- Office Supply Companies
- Local Government Officials
- Insurance Companies

Next, learn how to leverage these industry contacts to their utmost potential by practicing the following list of helpful networking tips:

12 Networking Tips

- Begin networking with people with whom you feel most comfortable (business acquaintances, current associates, etc.)
- Connect to your passion
- Volunteer to help others
- Recognize and deal with aspects of networking that bother you the most
- Create a structured plan and stick to it
- Set goals and be disciplined about achieving them

- Make calls when your energy is highest

- Take time to replenish yourself

- Practice what to say before you call, perhaps even jotting down the important points you want to mention

- Practice the process with a low priority organization or in an area where you feel you have nothing to lose before "taking it live"

- Don't be afraid to ask; all they can say is "no"

- Each time you succeed, take it to a higher level

5 Benefits of the CD Business Card

Chances are that while networking, and in your day-to-day business dealings, you will use your business card. Yet did you know that the most effective business card today is the CD Business Card? CD Business Cards not only provide standard business card information on the face of the CD, but they can also deliver volumes of information to the recipient that can be "viewed" on standard computers anywhere. In addition:

- CD cards can hold up to 25 photo images—the benefit of that feature alone is invaluable.

- CD cards can link to your "live" Website, enabling the viewer to access volumes of targeted information.

- You can install a PowerPoint presentation, Word Documents, Excel Files, etc., on your CD card.

- CD business cards can deliver a personal audio message, supported by a vibrant color opening page, company logo, and soundtrack.

- CD business cards are cost effective, attention-getting marketing tools.

12 Ways to Use Traditional Business Cards Wisely

If, however, you still use standard business cards, here are some unique twists and turns to an old song and dance that might turn those wallet fillers into wallet wonders:

- **Make your business card useful**. These days, business cards can be turned into everything from magnets to letter openers, meaning your card could be somewhere prominent, instead of lining the wastepaper basket!

- **Make it noticeable**. Something as simple as a different color, paper weight, or marbled texture can make your card stand out from the crowd.

- **Use both hands**. Make a statement by using both hands to present your business card. It's a small—but effective—trick.

- **Ask and you shall receive**. When it's too awkward to give away your card, ask for one. Chances are, they'll ask for your card in return.

- **Introduce yourself with your card**. Any time you meet someone new, hand them you business card.

- **Include your card with all correspondence**. From general correspondence to newsletters, you never know when—or where— a new tenant might come from.

- **Develop a system**. This applies for both carrying and collecting business cards. For filing purposes, decide which way is better for you to remember potential contacts, by industry, last name, etc.

- **Sign of the times.** Always write a brief message on a business card before handing it to someone.

- **Use a picture.** Put a recent photo of yourself on your card, especially in a "relationship" business such as commercial real estate. It will help your prospect relate to you as a person.

- **Phone home.** Highlight your telephone number by putting it in bold text or in a larger size than other numbers.

- **Signify freedom.** If you have a toll-free number, be sure to put it on your card, and label it as such. Some people may not recognize the toll-free prefix.

- **Cover both sides.** If possible, add to the value of your card by printing on both sides. Include useful information related to your industry, such as "fast facts" or useful statistics.

7 Tips for Remembering a Person's Name

No matter how many opportunities you may have for networking each week, none of them will ever pan out if you can't remember a prospect's name! This sales skill is one of the most basic of the Top Performer's arsenal, and here are seven ways to help add it to your own:

- As you are introduced, focus on the person you are meeting.
- Concentrate solely on that person for as long as you can.
- Scan the person's face or body for an unusual or distinctive feature.
- Repeat the person's name out loud.
- Link a distinctive facial or other physical feature with the name as you repeat it.
- Glance back at the person a few times to reinforce the link between their name and the mental picture you have created for them.
- At the end of the day write down the names of all the people you met and the mental picture you associate with them, perhaps on the back of each of their business cards.

"Trading" off of Trade Associations

Another valuable source of untapped networking opportunities is trade associations. Becoming a member of a local trade association can prove to be a valuable resource and a viable part of your network as you establish yourself as *the* real estate expert for their specific needs. More than likely, existing members of the trade association are all members whose area of expertise is directly related to the industry. By becoming a member and establishing yourself as *the* real estate expert for their association, you will not only be able to provide valuable insight into the real estate issues relative to their industry, you will ultimately be looked upon as their real estate advisor, from which fee service and transactions can result.

For example: If you are a broker of retail space, it would naturally benefit you to participate in the local Restaurant Association. How? Simple: Food courts provide space for parasite locations such as fast food outlets in regional malls and strip centers. Parasite stores provide a guaranteed high traffic area with a small rental space. Local members of this useful trade association are usually the owners/franchisees that make the final decision in the site selection, and a working relationship with them could mean untapped sales from an unlikely source.

Your participation in any targeted trade association can help you learn about the needs and concerns of its members. For instance, in the above example, our broker for retail space learned how profitable it could be to develop a working knowledge of restaurants, including new trends in the industry, such as co-branding (a donut shop and a sandwich concept sharing the same restaurant), smaller dinner houses (Fridays, Chili's, etc.), restaurants (for small towns), and unique sites for branded chains, such as those found on riverboats, on military bases, and in stadiums. All of this vital information may have remained untapped if the broker in our example had overlooked the valuable resource afforded him by simply looking into the local Restaurant Association.

13 Guidelines for Working with Trade Organizations

To make the most of networking with these plentiful—and profitable—trade associations, follow these thirteen simple guidelines:

- Identify various local and national groups by consulting the Encyclopedia of Associations.

- Attend a few local meetings to determine whether the real estate needs of the targeted association are relevant to your business purposes.

- Start out slowly, and establish trust. Begin by simply doing things that need to be done, such as organizing a monthly meeting, getting the announcements printed, helping to set up a trade fair or golf outing, etc. (These may not be glorious or even immediately beneficial tasks, but you will have an inside track on developing relationships with some of the association's most influential members, a powerful source of networking at its best.)

- Work on memorable introductions and building relationships rather than simply *selling*.

- Offer to speak on real estate issues related to the association— make the presentation meaningful and relevant.

- Keep track of whom you have met with a logical system, be it collecting business cards, Email addresses, checking off names on membership rosters, etc.

- Write a brief article for their newsletter or local publication.

- Be cooperative with others who are there to market themselves as well.

- Find reasons to re-establish contact with prospective tenants after the meeting.

- Follow up after the meeting.

- Get to know the staff of a particular organization, and zero in on the friendliest—or most efficient—contact person.

- Participate regularly for maximum exposure.

- Pick the associations you work with carefully to avoid wasting your time, and theirs.

Public Relations in Commercial Real Estate

Public relations can be a cost-effective alternative to—or even in addition to—the traditional advertising campaign of print and broadcast ads. Profitable public relation efforts include such promotional activities as speaking engagements, trade show presence, and media coverage.

7 Tips for Getting Good PR Coverage

Getting good media coverage can be easy, *if* you adhere to the following 7 steps:

- **Be Cordial (and don't give gifts)**. Magazine and newspaper editors, already a suspicious lot, will see them as bribes and thus avoid giving you coverage.

- **Be Clear and Succinct**. Getting straight to the point is the key with all press releases. Tell your story, give it some good context, and get it out. Let editors decide how and where to use it.

- **Have a Sustained Effort**. Public relations can't be a one-time thing for *any* company. It has to be an effort that is built up over time and eventually gains a steady momentum.

- **Tell the Truth**. Always be honest with the media.

- **Lose the Ego**. Don't allow the vanity of a big-talking CEO to get in the way of good PR.

- **Research, Research, Research**. Make sure your PR people thoroughly understand the publications they are courting. Know the editors and create relationships with these knowledgeable professionals so they can feel free to call them at any time.

- **Be Timely**. Too many companies sit on their good stories, waiting to release them at trade shows or conferences. If you have something good to tell, tell it immediately.

(Adapted from *Sales & Marketing* Magazine)

The Company Newsletter

Many successful companies have found that publishing a newsletter, be it weekly, monthly, or quarterly, is a profitable networking tool well worth the expense of maintaining a quality publication on a regular basis.

Your customers will benefit from your expertise, news items, lists, and services, and as a result you will build a loyal and captive audience for your services that could number well into the thousands by the end of your first year "in publication."

10 Reasons to Publish a Company Newsletter

- It can provide an informative, soft sell introduction to prospects.

- It can provide prospects with information they will, can, and *should* use.

- It can keep you in touch on a regular basis, without being perceived as a pest.

- It can keep your customers up-to-date on your services and products.

- It can remind prospects, past tenants, and colleagues that you exist and may even motivate them to contact you.

- It can demonstrate your expertise in a field.

- It can educate tenants when they have no time to educate themselves.

- It can provide an opportunity or forum for you to explain complicated products, services, or offers.

- It can trigger more sales by providing tips on how to use your services.

- It does wonders to enhance your credibility.

7 Newsletter Pointers

Today's newsletters run the gamut from glossy printouts to digital e-zines, but whatever your chosen medium, the desired outcome is the same: more business, more sales, and more *profit*. Here are seven timely tips for writing—and maintaining—a profitable company newsletter:

- Start with a quarterly newsletter, and add more pages—or another issue—if necessary.

- Steer clear of company news and focus on information that will actually help the tenant, such as trends analysis, news items, tips, checklists, calendars, etc.

- Survey readers to gauge their reactions to the content and design, and make reasonable changes accordingly.

- Post the newsletter on the company's Website, if you have one. It is a minimal investment and an easy way to reach more prospects. (This also makes it easier to offer an electronic version of your newsletter, which further builds a targeted Email marketing list when you send the e-newsletter out each week/month/quarter.)

- Get tenant testimonials for content. They love reading about themselves. However, make sure it is accurate and have them sign off on the content before it is published.

- Invite submissions from tenants and readers. This makes your job easier, and their pride larger.

- *Never* charge for your newsletter.

Selling Skills for the Commercial Real Estate Practitioner

Technology, techniques, and other tools are all just that—tools to help the Top Performer stay at the top. But the actual *skills* needed to sustain powerful and regular sales require further attention here as well. These include building confidence, establishing relationships, cold calling skills, ways to be memorable, listening skills, establishing trust, getting to the decision maker, questioning techniques and so much more . . .

Determining Need:

C.E.N.U.L.A.R.R.

One of the most vital sales skills unique to the *Systems for Success* toolbox is one of our most effective tools for determining need. **C.E.N.U.L.A.R.R.** is a tool that will allow the sales professional to determine what the needs of the customer *really* are. When each of **C.E.N.U.L.A.R.R.**'s eight questions have been answered, it will help you uncover the unarticulated and un-served needs of any current or prospective tenant:

CAUSES	EXPECTATIONS	NEEDS	URGENCY	LOYALTY	AUTHORITY	RESOURCE	REVENUE
Pain	Picture	Solution	Timing	Relationship	Decision	Credit	Cash Flow
							Account
							Transaction
1		2		3		4	5

Copyright © The Lipsey Company - www.lipseyco.com

Causes: Why does something need to be done? What pain or discomfort is going to be resolved?

Expectations: What is the end result of the project and costs (customer paints a mental picture)?

Needs: As opposed to a requirement (emotional vs. specific).

Urgency: When does the project need to be done? Why does it need to be done then?

Loyalty: What is our relationship to this person?

Authority: Who can authorize this project and what are the steps to getting an okay?

Revenue: What type of revenue can you generate that is non-traditional revenue?

Resource: Does the company or department have the financial ability to do the project?

3 Solutions in Probing for Needs

Probing for needs is a vital step toward giving the tenant what he wants, and establishing a sale that is mutually beneficial. A mistake of even the most experienced business developer? Describing how the professional will help before adequate information is gathered on the prospect's needs.

To avoid this sales hurdle, here are three simple solutions for probing for these all-important tenant needs.

1. **Begin with open-ended questions**. Questions that don't lend themselves to a multiple-choice answer keep the tenant talking—and you learning. The more a tenant says, the more you are likely to learn. Letting a tenant off the hook with "yes" or "no" answers is the sure way to missing out on the background information that is so crucial to a final sale.

2. **Focus on issues that matter**. Small talk is essential to building tenant rapport, but remember to keep steering the tenant back to what matters. Your information gathering may be a stop-start approach peppered with everything from last night's basketball scores to the morning's weather, but as long as you continually reroute the conversation in the direction of a sale, your long and winding road may just lead to success.

3. **Narrow your focus toward the close**. Always be on the lookout for "closure." Resolutions are the endgame of every sales call, and finding out what the tenant wants is the only way to actually give it to him. Look for narrow topics among the big picture, and focus on those as you continue to probe for vital information.

How to Ask the Perfect Question

The technique of asking—and answering—questions is nothing less than the very heart of a sales call. Without questions, you'll have no answers. Without answers, you'll have no sales. Questions are to sales what breathing is to life. If you fail to ask them, you will die. If you ask them incorrectly, your death won't be immediate, but it's just as inevitable. If you ask them correctly, the answer is . . . a sale.

The 3 Stages of Setting up a Real Estate Question

Stage 1: Make a factual statement that can't be refuted.

Example: "In the last six years, consumers have responded more favorably to outdoor malls than those indoors."

Stage 2: Make a personal observation that reflects your experience and creates credibility.

Example: "Last year alone, I placed 30 tenants in high-traffic outside locations."

Stage 3: Ask an open-ended question that incorporates the first two stages.

Example: "What can I do to place you in the most beneficial location for your business?"

17 Surface Questions to Ask a Real Estate Buyer

Questioning a tenant is a lot like drilling for oil: Merely scratching the surface will never get you there. But you've got to start somewhere. The following is a targeted list of "surface questions" to get you started on that next sales geyser:

1.) Establish Issues:

- Please give me the background on your situation.
- Please tell me about your reason for asking me to meet with you.

2.) Establish Cause:

- How did it start?
- How did it happen?

3.) Establish Urgency/Complication:

- This has been going on for some time. Why hasn't it been resolved?
- Why is this on your mind now?

4.) Establish Scope:

- What needs to be dealt with now?

5.) Validate Buyer's Diagnosis:

- What indications do you have that this is happening?

6.) Establish Company Value/Implication:

- What will happen if the problem persists?
- What difference would it make to have it fixed?

7.) Establish Personal Value:

- What is your personal interest in this problem?

8.) Establish Other Participants' Values:

- Please tell me a little about their interest in the project?

9.) Establish Desired Outcome:

- What would you like to see happen?

- A year from now, if this problem were fixed, what would be different?

10.) Establish Performance Measures:

- How much do you expect to save?

- When do you need this completed?

- If we gave you a (plan, methodology, etc.) would that help you?

11.) Establish Project Size:

- How many employees do you have?

- How many feet will it be?

12.) Establish Process:

- Please tell me a little about choosing a (consultant, lawyer, architect, accountant)?

13.) Identify Participants:

- Who else is on your committee?

- What is the CEO's role in this?

14.) Establish Timing:

- When do you expect to make a decision?
- When do we start?

15.) Understand Your Relationship with the Buyer:

- How did you hear about my firm?
- Why did you call me?
- What issues will your selection of a professional hinge on?
- Are you considering other firms?
- How would you compare us to the competition?

16.) Uncover Impediments:

- Please give me an update on the project.

17.) Determine the Readiness to Close:

- When do we start?
- Where do we go from here?
- Would you like a proposal?

9 Questions for your Question

The best way to learn valuable information is to NOT sound like you're asking a lot of questions. A good Q & A session should sound less like an interrogation—and more like a friendly conversation. To that end, here are nine tips for asking relevant questions, without appearing like you're asking *too many*:

- Cushion the questions: "Would you permit me a few questions?"

- Start questions with an action verb, such as "tell," "describe," "give," etc.

- Keep questions open-ended to keep buyers talking.

- Is the question clear and concise? Does the prospect understand the question?

- Does the question require productive thinking before the prospect can formulate a response?

- Do you appear to be more knowledgeable than your competitors by probing in new areas?

- Does the question lead the prospect (and you) to draw from past experience?

- Does the question relate directly to the prospect's objectives?

- Does the question draw information from the prospect that helps you make the sale easier?

9 Reasons Why Top Producers Ask Questions

- Questions focus on the buyer, not you or your product.

- Questions uncover pain.

- Questions represent positive psychological strokes.

- Questions are more conversational, natural, and less manipulative than a prepared presentation.

- Questions relieve your pressure and stress.

- Questions ensure that the buyer does most of the talking.

- Questions give you a chance to think.

- Questions minimize the risk you will say something you might later regret.

- Questions commit the buyer.

14 Powerful Lead-in Questions

Never underestimate the power of a good lead-in question. And while the best lead-ins are those uniquely tailored to each tenant—loaded with specifics based on market research and quality listening skills—here are thirteen powerful lead-ins to get you started:

- "What do you look for...?"
- "What have you found...?"
- "How do you propose...?"
- "What has been your experience...?"
- "How have you successfully used...?"
- "How do you determine...?"
- "Why is that a deciding factor...?"
- "What makes you choose...?"
- "What do you like about...?"
- "What would you change about...? (Do not say, "What *don't* you like about...?")
- "Are there other factors...?"
- "What does your competitor do about...?"
- "How do your customers react to...?"
- "How would you describe....?"

(**Source**: Adapted from *The Sales Bible* by Jeffrey H. Gitomer)

Effective Listening

While probing a tenant with calculated questions is one tool for the Top Performer, these sales achievers also realize that you can learn an enormous amount by simply being *quiet*. You also learn more by listening rather than speaking. Effective listening leads to sales, and lots of them! Listening is arguably the most important aspect of the selling process, yet it is the one skill that usually receives the least amount of attention . . .

16 Skill-Building Techniques to Become a Better Listener

Every Top Performer knows that good selling skills start—and end—with good *listening* skills. To that end, try the following sixteen skill-building techniques to become a better listener:

- Make positive eye contact.
- Focus your attention on the words and their meaning.
- Limit distractions.
- Visualize the situation being described.
- Visualize your response or solution before responding.
- Listen with an open mind.
- Listen to the content.
- Write things down.
- Verify the situation (sometimes) before giving feedback.
- Qualify the situation with questions.
- Don't interrupt the next time you think you know the answer.
- While eating in a group, don't talk for the first half hour.
- Ask questions to clarify.

- Ask questions to show interest or concern.

- Ask questions to get more information or learn.

- Ask yourself, "Are you listening to the other person the same way you want to be listened to?"

(**Source**: *The Sales Bible* by Jeffery H. Gitomer)

A Listening Quiz

Determine your Listening IQ with our helpful test. Answer each statement of the following Listening Quiz with either "Rarely," "Sometimes," or "Always":

R	**S**	**A**	I allow speakers to complete sentences.
R	**S**	**A**	I make sure I understand the other person before responding.
R	**S**	**A**	I listen for the important points.
R	**S**	**A**	I try to understand the speaker's feelings.
R	**S**	**A**	I visualize the solution before speaking.
R	**S**	**A**	I am in control, relaxed, and calm when listening.
R	**S**	**A**	I use listening noises ("um," "gee," "I see," "oh").
R	**S**	**A**	I take notes when someone else is speaking.
R	**S**	**A**	I listen with an open mind.
R	**S**	**A**	I listen even if the other person is not interesting.
R	**S**	**A**	I listen even if the other person is a jerk.
R	**S**	**A**	I look at the person I'm listening to.
R	**S**	**A**	I am patient when I listen.
R	**S**	**A**	I ask questions to be sure I understand.
R	**S**	**A**	I have no distractions when I listen.

Now, add up the total number of "Always" responses you circled:

_____

- **If you answered "Always" from 14-16 times:** You are excellent.

- **If you answered "Always" from 11-13 times:** You are good, but need help in a few areas.

- **If you answered "Always" from 7-10 times:** You are fair, probably think you know it all, and could increase your income significantly with skill-building help.

- **If you answered "Always" from 4-6 times:** You are poor, not listening at all.

- **If you answered "Always" from 1-3 times:** You are ear dead—or brain dead—or in need of a hearing aid.

8 Steps to Better Listening Skills

- Get into a listening posture
- Take notes
- Screen out distractions
- Limit your talking
- Listen for content
- Check for non-verbals
- Keep the buyer talking
- Prove that you listened

Remember the 2 Rules of Effective Listening:

(In this order)

- Listen with the intent to understand.
- Listen with the intent to offer an intelligent response.

10 Quick Phrases to Keep Tenants Talking

The less a tenant talks, the more work you have to do. The more a tenant talks, the more you learn—without even trying. Therefore, Top Performers know that to listen better—and learn *more*—it is crucial that the tenant keep talking. They accomplish this feat with verbal cues that signal a tenant to continue conversing, even when they may be reluctant to talk. Here are the Top 10:

- "And . . . "
- "And then what happened?"
- "What else?"
- "What was that experience like?"
- "Can you tell me more about that?"
- "And how did that work?"
- "How do you feel about that?"
- "Can you give me any details?"
- "What makes you sure?"
- "How do you measure that?"

Selling to the Decision Maker

Selling at the corporate level, where decisions are made, requires significant intelligence, knowledge, maturity, and steadfastness. The decision to target this level should not be taken lightly—there are no quick and easy sales here! Selling at this level could take years to come to fruition, but the payoff is worthwhile.

Most top executives claim that a salesperson's knowledge of their companies' business is low or very low, and state that most salespeople cannot move past the obsession with selling features and benefits—that they resist attempts to shift the focus to customer needs and business solutions.

Today's top producer knows that if the product/service they are selling does not in some way positively affect the tenant's bottom line, or increase productivity, or otherwise add value to their business, there *is* no sale. The following are a few tips on how to prepare to sell to the decision-maker.

- Research and understand what is important to the decision-maker. Nothing establishes credibility more than your willingness to invest significant time and energy researching the prospect's company, their current needs, and vision for the future. This establishes you as a true sales professional.

- Understand that those at the "C" level think and operate at a much bigger, broader, and more global level. Naturally, this is a different selling approach, and a fixed, shortsighted agenda will not sell.

- Align the prospect's corporate vision and strategic initiatives with your selling strategy by incorporating *their* vision or mission in *your* presentation.

- Investigate current corporate initiatives and/or business issues.

- Be sure you can deliver and execute on the ideas an executive shares with you. After all, that is the unwritten expectation.

- Don't ignore mid-level executives—the real buying often takes place at this level.

- While you may not always talk to the CEO—the CEO may refer you to a lower level—this carries much weight and a certain degree of importance.

- Don't put limits on who you call; it is much easier to call on the more senior level executive and be redirected to one slot lower in the chain of command than to start at the bottom and never get that far.

- Don't put limits on yourself when you interact with the decision-maker: be candid, be direct, and most importantly, be yourself.

- Understand that in today's changing corporate structure a new network model exists, one where everyone talks to everyone else. CEOs are thus more accessible and responsive to outside sources and information.

- CEOs no longer have tenure—their positions are now performance-based—so they can't afford to ignore you and often welcome information relevant to the corporate vision or a pet project.

- Those at the "C" level are looking for you to align and collaborate with them. Therefore, bring things to their attention that they might not normally understand.

- Remember, do not focus on selling Features and Benefits; focus on Selling Solutions, and don't show up for the appointment if you don't have a viable business solution to offer.

8 Places to Find the Information Needed to Sell to the Decision-Maker

Information is a vital component of your ability to sell to the decision-maker. Extensive research must be undertaken before you approach your prospect so that every aspect of your communication is relevant to the prospect's issues and objectives. Only with this level of research and knowledge will you be able to formulate viable solutions designed to enhance the prospect's business. The following are seven of the most valuable sources of information to leverage as you research your prospect:

- Corporate Websites

- Annual Reports

- Contacts Inside the Company

- Hoovers Online Business Network

- Business Journals

- The CEO's most recent speech (these are a great source of information)

- Call the Executive Assistant and ask for copies of recent articles (they are often happy to provide them)

- Dunn & Broadstreet

8 Ways to Build Credibility and Establish Trust

The key to selling to the decision maker is to build credibility and establish trust. This is best achieved when you take the eight following steps:

- Demonstrate knowledge of the prospect's business
- Understand and align with their vision
- Understand the dynamics of their "team"
- Become an ally of every individual on the team
- Have knowledge of their key issues and challenges
- Show how your product/service helps them achieve their goals
- Demonstrate how you have created value for similar companies
- Prove your ethics with action

10 Commandments of a Commercial Real Estate Top Producer

In this industry, all Top Performers live by a code of rules, a cannon of laws, a set of commandments, which are as follows:

- **Have Excellent Communication Skills**: Impeccable oral and written communication skills are a must for a successful sales career. This includes good telephone etiquette and strong presentation skills.

- **Have Initiative and Self-discipline**: A convincing product presentation requires continual study to update your knowledge. Keep current with your own products as well as your customers' operations. Be punctual for tenant appointments and ensure your availability (at least on the phone) whenever the customer seeks you.

- **Have Persistence**: A sale is rarely closed the first time a presentation is made. A long series of callbacks may be required, especially if the sale involves heavy capital expenditure. If the buying decision is an important one, the approval of several senior executives may be required before the order can be placed. This often involves a lengthy period of negotiation, but if you continue your sales efforts with persistence and tact, you may be rewarded.

- **Make a Great Presentation**: A smart, business-like appearance will go a long way in helping you achieve your objective.

- **Have the Ability to Communicate at all Levels**: Since the buying decision within a corporation may be influenced by a number of executives in the customer's firm, a single sale may take you from the line manager to the CEO. You must be prepared to speak the language of each.

- **Have the Ability to Plan**: Successful sales professionals not only plan their daily and weekly schedule but often their individual calls.

- **Be Friendly and Considerate**: A customer's strong patronage toward an existing supplier/vendor is difficult to break down. To build your own relationship you need to be attentive to ways in which you can help the prospect and generally be liked by the people with whom you are negotiating.

- **Have Integrity**: Integrity and honesty do not preclude enthusiasm about your product, service, or company, but what you say about these things should be provable. Make promises that are demonstrable. Misrepresentation by implication or omission destroys buyer confidence.

- **Have an Eagerness to Learn**: In a dynamic environment, new technologies become obsolete in a short span of time. Given this scenario, you cannot afford to stop learning. Stay up to date on issues that concern your products, industry, and customer segments.

- **Have a Systematic Approach**: A clear focus backed by a sound strategy will support you in your endeavors. Without a systematic and methodical way of attacking the market, your energies will be dissipated.

9 Ways to Keep Your Commercial Real Estate Selling Skills Sharp

Selling skills are only useful if they are utilized, effectively and over time. Keeping your selling skills sharp is an ongoing process that requires an investment of time, effort and, often, money. Here are nine ways to keep your selling skills sharp:

- **Start a personal library**. No Top Performer thinks he or she knows it all. Likewise, you should waste no time in beginning a personal library of books that would be beneficial to you, and your business. From self-help to sales, commercial real estate to marketing, good business books are a sound investment in any Top Performer's "book."

- **Subscribe**. Don't limit your business reading to books, however. Keep up to date on the latest sales techniques, technology, and market trends by subscribing to one or more of the industry's best magazines or journals. Then read them each month!

- **Read**. Having a library and several magazine subscriptions may look good to office visitors, but they'll only increase sales if you know what's inside. Set aside 5-7 hours a week for business reading, from the latest business bestsellers to your trade journals. When being informed on a national trend or local event seals the deal, you'll be glad you did!

- **Listen in your car**. Don't have time for "quiet reading?" Don't waste it listening to hit songs in your car. Instead, buy or checkout business books on audio tape or CD and make your daily drive time worthwhile.

- **Go mobile**. Even Top Performers are often kept waiting. Stay current on the latest business trends by always bringing reading material, books or magazines, with you in your briefcase, purse, or satchel.

- **Stay technologically current**. Don't fall behind the times by being a "techno-snob." Balking at new technology is one sure way to fall behind the times.

- **Form a "Support Group."** Not just for networking, but for bouncing ideas off of each other, venting frustrations, picking minds, and a host of other beneficial duties that can all be performed as easily over a happy hour buffet as a boardroom table.

- **Keep an open mind**. To ideas, to people, to technology, to trends, to everything. Don't hop on every bandwagon, but at least listen to what they're playing!

- **Attend at least one personal development seminar every year.** New ideas are often best expressed live and in person. Get energized once a year or, if you can afford the cost or the time away from the office, as often as possible.

15 Negative Words (and Their Positive Alternatives)

Part and parcel of being a Top Performer is paying attention to even the most minute of details. This means watching every word that comes out of your mouth. Specifically, Top Performers recognize—and avoid—words that could be considered "negative," using positive alternatives instead. Here is a helpful list of both:

Negative	Positive
Cost	Total Investment
Down Payment	Initial Investment
Monthly Payment	Monthly Investment
Contract	Agreement
Buy	Own
Sell	Enjoy Owning
Sign	Endorse
Pitch	Demonstration
Deal	Package
Credit Application	Account Information
Problem	Challenge
Objections	Areas of Concern
Cheaper	More Economical
Prospect	Future Tenant
Appointment	Visit

8 Ways to be Memorable

Sales don't always result how—and especially when—you want them to. The best way to set yourself up for a future sale is to be memorable *right now*. Here are a few great ways to start making a lasting impression:

- An impressive business card
- Hand delivery
- Deliver more than you promised
- Fast delivery
- Personal thank you cards
- After-hours service
- Personal attention before, during, and AFTER the sale
- Deliver a personalized gift of thanks (possible book of interest, etc.)

8 Great Relationship Rules for Commercial Practitioners

To become a Top Performer, you must be able to sell someone twice, to refer to someone in a friendly way, a sincere way, and a way that emphasizes serving first—and selling second. To accomplish that lofty goal, here is a list of "rules" for relationship building at the highest level:

- Say it in terms of what the customer wants, needs, and understands.
- Build a friendship.
- Build a relationship shield that no competitor can pierce.
- Gain confidence.
- Have fun.
- Never get caught *selling*.
- Question (with the right questions).
- Listen (with the intent to understand).

3 Short Steps to Building Long-term Relationships with Your Real Estate Clients

Every Top Performer knows that selling is really about building relationships. That is why the best salesperson you know will almost always be referred to as a "people person." They're not just *selling* to their tenants, they're relating to them in an enjoyable and mutually beneficial way. Therefore, in a fitting end to this section on selling, we remind you that selling *is* relating by providing you with *3 Short Steps to Building Long-term Relationships*:

- **Step 1**: Establish the short-term metrics by which you can evaluate your efforts. For example, increased cross-selling, decreased processing, faster cycle times.

- **Step 2**: Identify a small group of customers with whom to begin your efforts—possibly those who may be more receptive to your initiative.

- **Step 3**: Define specific projects that can be measured against one of the criteria above and that will have an effect on the customers you've identified for the effort.

Michael J. Lipsey

PART TWO:

PRESENTING SKILLS FOR COMMERCIAL REAL ESTATE PRACTITIONERS

Michael J. Lipsey

Introduction

A good business presentation sells either a thing or an idea. Otherwise, it is merely a discussion or a story. It takes knowledge, talent, and skill to make a true sales presentation to the decision makers at the top level of corporate America. After all, making such a presentation involves much more than convincing this elite brand of customer to *buy* your service.

Bear in mind that the presentation is only a small, though important, part of a sale. You have researched the marketplace. The property or service is positioned to meet the customer's needs. You have developed this prospect and created a relationship with some or all of the buyers. Now it is time to make the presentation and *close* the sale.

Unfortunately, the best-qualified person does not always win—but the best presentation *can* make the difference.

Accordingly, the *Systems for Success* **Presenting** Program blends soft skills, such as how to understand and then fulfil the needs of your tenants, with hardcore sales skills designed to get you past the gate keepers and straight to the decision makers.

Here you will learn the five keys to making an effective sales presentation:

1. **Preparation**
2. **Knowing Your Audience**
3. **Visual Aids**
4. **Mechanics & Delivery**
5. **Public Speaking**

In the first section, *Preparation*, you will learn that without proper preparation, all the eye contact and flashy visual aids in the world won't make a difference. Here you'll find targeted, accessible, and easy-to-digest lists designed to help you research, organize, and rehearse your very next presentation, with ideas you can use right now. Today.

In the second section, *Knowing Your Audience*, you will discover how to be more convincing by tailoring your presentation to each specific audience. We will help you learn to anticipate and prepare for tough objections and present winning solutions.

Next, in our comprehensive *Visual Aids* section, you will learn the skills and technology that will make an incredible difference in your very next presentation. From low-tech to high-tech, you will finally understand the art of selecting and presenting effective visual aids, slides, and charts. Learn the effects of color in the background of your slide presentation, and the advantages and disadvantages of many of today's various visual solutions.

Then, in *Mechanics & Delivery*, you arrive at the very heart of a sales presentation. Here you will discover various tips and tactics designed to share your message more effectively. From ways to overcome your fear of presenting to tips for solving the age-old solution of making eye contact. List after list of only the most valuable tips and tactics make up this invaluable section designed to prepare you for nearly any form of successful sales presentation.

Finally, in *Public Speaking*, you will be able to capitalize on the advice given in our previous chapter, **SELLING**, for branching out and addressing trade groups and seminar audiences, possibly even giving keynotes before you're through!

Understanding how to effectively use the latest technology on the market and combining the advanced speaking skills we teach you will enable you to differentiate yourself from the competition.

The *Systems for Success* training program focuses on every phase of a winning presentation. With our *Systems* firmly-entrenched and geared toward today's competitive marketplace, your speaking *Success* is virtually guaranteed . . .

Preparing for a Presentation

A powerful presentation is the result of thorough preparation. Whether making a presentation informally, across the desk from a customer, or formally, during a meeting among key decision-makers, each presentation must be geared toward fulfilling the needs of the tenant. Furthermore, it should take into consideration key information obtained in the earlier steps of the sales process.

The better you know your subject matter and the more prepared you are for each particular prospect, the more comfortable you will be during your presentation and the more effective your presentation will ultimately be.

There is no *substitute* for good preparation. The importance of sufficient preparation for a presentation cannot be overstated. A well-prepared presentation is the single most persuasive tool in your sales arsenal. Before making your presentation, the following steps in the planning stage will help ensure the effectiveness of your presentation.

- **Research**: Conduct research using the resources we've provided and gather the resulting information into a rough draft of your presentation materials.

- **The Selection Process**: Next you need to select the information you will use, and refine it to better suit your needs. Facts and figures are fine, but how much is *too* much? How many examples and illustrations do you need to make your point? These are all helpful questions to guide you through this process.

- **Decide on the format**: How will you present your speech? What tools will you use? Will there be a question and answer period? How long will the presentation be?

- **Know the Material**: Read, study, and learn the material you will be speaking on several times until you are thoroughly comfortable with it. To feel *confident* about your material, you need to be *knowledgeable* about your material.

- **Have Landmarks**: Whether your speech is four minutes or four hours long, be sure to leave yourself a few "crumbs" along the way. Easy to remember titles, or several recaps throughout will help you orient yourself with the contents of your presentation.

- **Rehearse**: There is no substitute for an effective rehearsal of your presentation. Giving several test runs of your presentation is a great way to weed out words that become stumbling blocks, or phrases that are awkward.

- **Have a Backup Plan**: Note cards, good visual aids, laser pointers, even an impromptu question and answer session halfway through your presentation are all effective ways to derail a presentation that is slowly going sour. Having a backup plan for those inevitable awkward moments isn't just a good strategy, it just makes good sense.

Creating **The Presentation**

The initial part of the presenting process involves creating the actual presentation itself. Whether it's five minutes with middle management or a formal review for the CEO, each sales presentation must be designed for maximum effect, beginning with step one: the *creation* of the presentation itself.

There are four steps to creating an effective sales presentation:

- **Determine Your Objective**
- **Review Customer Needs, Benefits, Requirements & Solutions**
- **Create a Unique Package**
- **Organize Your Presentation**

Determine Your Real Estate Presentation Objectives

Many inexperienced presenters focus on the presentation itself, versus the *message* you want to deliver. Determining the objectives of your presentation at the beginning of the process is one easy way to avoid this tragic mistake. There are three steps to determining your objective:

1. **Determine the specific objective(s) of your presentation.** What is it, specifically, you are trying to achieve with this presentation? Who are you trying to reach?

2. **Determine the solution you will present.** Do you intend to convince the customer that there is one best answer or do you want to explain the options you can offer?

3. **Determine the desired end result.** Are you informing them to prepare for some future activity? Is it your goal to close the sale?

3 Ways to Outline your Objectives

Many a desired objective has been left out of an ineffective presentation due to poor planning. Your objectives for any given presentation should be as detailed, specific, and, more importantly, as *measurable* as possible. For instance, what *measurable* results can the tenant expect as a result of your presentation, or your service? What will be the end *result*? What will the *specific* outcome be?

Giving your objectives definite meaning will not only make them more concrete to you, but to your audience as well. The following sample objective statements are designed to illustrate how a general objective can be made more specific—or measurable—to better meet desired results:

General Objective: Discuss the customer's request to complete the project early.

Specific Objective: Generate a step-by-step plan to finish the project by May 1st.

General Objective: Reduce budget.

Specific Objective: Ways to reduce overtime costs by 15%.

General Objective: Improve corporate communications.

Specific Objective: Develop a four-page company newsletter by June 1.

Once you have determined your objectives, it is imperative that you outline them to facilitate their inclusion in the eventual presentation. Here are some ways to avoid overlooking your main objective(s):

3 Questions for Establishing your Objectives

Use the following questions to help you establish the objectives for your next presentation:

1. Who asked me to speak and what is the subject matter?

   _____

   _____

   _____

2. What objective(s) do I want to achieve with this audience?

   _____

   _____

   _____

3. What is in it for *them*?

_____

_____

_____

Review Customer Needs, Benefits, Requirements, and Solutions

Before preparing your presentation, review your notes and files and make sure that:

- Customer needs have been determined

- Consequences and payoffs have been explored

- Options have been evaluated and solutions developed

Your goal is to obtain your pre-determined objective (Step 1), and ultimately, a commitment from the customer. Before you begin, find out if anything has changed since you last spoke with your tenant; there may be some last minute information that will have a bearing on what you say in your presentation.

Spend time at the beginning of the presentation to review the previous meeting, recall your last conversation, renew trust and rapport, and get the customer to take an active role in your presentation.

Throughout your presentation you have the opportunity to fulfill your tenant's needs. To do this, you must build a relationship with everyone in the room and you must begin your presentation with an *Opening Benefit Statement* that indicates to everyone present that you understand and are prepared to address their needs.

Defining Your Opening Benefit Statement

During the initial stage of the presentation you will present your opening remarks. Maintain good eye contact and an open, friendly, manner. During this phase, you will:

- Review the tenant's needs
- State the objectives for your presentation
- Give an Opening Benefit/Solution Statement to establish expectation of value to be received.

4 Steps of the *Opening Benefit/Solution Statement*

The opening benefit statement indicates to the prospect that you already have a solution to their needs. It tells the tenant why they should invest time in listening to your presentation. The Opening Benefit/Solution Statement consists of four parts:

- A general need, indicating the need for a solution (client needs more space)

- A general feature or service which you and your company can provide

- The advantage of the general feature, i.e., "how it works"

- The general benefit which the client will derive from the feature you offer

Creating A Unique Package

An unspoken part of making an effective presentation is creating a unique package for each prospect or tenant. This can be accomplished in three ways:

- Based on your analysis and discussion of possible options with the Customer, create a package of products/services that will solve the problems, and/or meet the needs.

- Examine possible product enhancements, pricing/payoff options, delivery, etc.

- Differentiate yourself from the competition by presenting a uniquely tailored solution to the customer's needs.

Establishing Features & Benefits/Solutions

A further objective of creating a unique package is to provide your client with solutions in terms of features and benefits that relate directly to their identified need. This can be accomplished in three ways:

- Present details of the features and advantages of the benefits, point by point.

- There may be times when you might understand your client's needs better than he/she does, but if you cannot successfully tie the benefits/solutions of your product/service to those needs, you will reduce the chance of obtaining a commitment.

- Explain how the benefits of your solution can meet the client's needs.

4 Steps to Developing Your Presentation Content

Any good presentation goes through several drafts, and to get to a draft, it is important to develop your presentation content to the utmost effect. To do so, we suggest the following four steps:

- **Determine What You Are Going to Cover:** Most likely, this step will already be done for you. Be it a sales presentation or informative get-together for current tenants or future prospects, it is still important that you focus on the most important material to deliver.

- **Envision the Result**: To get where you want to go, you must first see what you want to accomplish. Envisioning the result is one sure way to get there. Don't spend time worrying about how well you'll do, spend time preparing for where you want to be—then get there with a great presentation.

- **Research. Research. Did We Mention, *Research*?** We've said it before, but we'll say it again: Research is the key to a good presentation. Research your latest sales material, research your audience, research your venue, research areas you don't feel knowledgeable enough about. But research just the same . . .

- **Choose Your Visual Aids**: Once you have your content written to the level of your satisfaction, it is time to select your visuals. Don't be pressured into using the "latest, greatest" system "everyone else" is using. Go with your gut and slowly add technology as you progress as a presenter. Just make sure your visuals say what you want, how you want, and that your audience can actually read them!

3 Tips for Editing Your Content for Impact

When you have finished writing your presentation draft, it is imperative that you carefully edit it for misspellings, typos, and grammatical errors. But before taking that final step, you should also make sure that you haven't just used proper grammar, but *effective* language as well. You want your presentation to be memorable, to pack a punch. In order to do so, try the following 3 tips:

- **Use descriptive words:** Don't say, "This is a new program." Say, "This is a *revolutionary* new program." Don't say, "Corporate is behind us." Say, "Corporate is *enthusiastic about* our revolutionary new program." Descriptive words are like seasonings: You don't want to add too many, but you want to add just enough.

- **Use active voice:** Don't say, "We were recently awarded with commercial real estate brokers of the year." Say, "*Real Estate Today* awarded us with their top honor!" Make everything active, using strong verbs instead of relying on the past tense.

- **Avoid jargon:** Don't say, "The New TX-5 is targeted for third quarter launch once the specs are complete." Say, "We're working on our latest technological breakthrough." Even though most of your audience will know your industry jargon, don't fall back on using it. Like good visual aids, a good presentation should be simple and stand alone. A good test for a jargon-free speech should be, "Would your mother understand what you are saying?"

The 4-Part Structure of a Presentation

As you're making preparations to give your next presentation, it is a good idea to keep in mind the structure of a presentation. This way, you are sure to stay focused and on target. Here are four ways to make the most out of a presentation's structure:

- **Tell Them What You Are Going to Say**: As sophisticated as they may seem, today's audiences still live in today's world. As such, their attention span is somewhat limited. To keep them focused and alert, tell them what you are going to say, broken down into no more than five parts or sections.

- **List What You Have Just Told Them**: On a flip-chart, slide, poster, or printed, individual agendas, list precisely those five points you've just told them you are going to touch on. Suggest that they mark them off, either mentally or physically, as you go along.

- **Recap What You Have Said Along the Way**: After finishing each point on your list of five, recap what you have just said. Build on these recaps as you progress through the presentation. For instance, after completing a discussion of part three, you should recap parts one through three, and so on.

- **Read The List When You're Done**: Some audience members take notes, others don't. To make sure your audience takes away what you've tried to give them, use one final recap to list the five topics, sections, points, or ideas you discussed.

Organize Your Presentation

"A well-organized presentation is a well-prepared presentation." Remember—and continually repeat—this important mantra as you get ready for your next opportunity to speak. Here are four ways we can help:

- Thoroughly prepare and organize your presentation materials as much ahead of time as possible.

- If your presentation involves any audiovisual equipment, try to familiarize yourself with the room to determine the best placement of your equipment, seating arrangements, etc. Check the equipment to make sure everything is in working order.

- The basic elements of your presentation should be well planned and rehearsed, such as opening, summarizing, providing solutions, exploring payoffs, and concluding.

- Practice your presentation so that you feel comfortable enough to throw away the script. Pay particular attention to your opening and closing statements, these are the most listened-to segments of your presentation.

Creating an Amazing Presentation Agenda in 10 Easy Steps

What did we ever do before agendas? An agenda is an important tool for a presenter because it enables the presenter to control the flow of the presentation. It also provides the audience with an overview of the activities to be completed. Below, you will find ten tips designed to help you create an "Amazing Agenda" for your next presentation.

- Distribute the agenda *before* the presentation.
- Discuss the agenda before you begin the presentation.
- Always have the date on the agenda, for future reference.
- Stick to **one** type of emphasis, such as bold, or italic, or underline; don't mix.
- Don't get too fancy; it's distracting and your audience won't appreciate it.
- If room permits, give an overview of key sections.
- Assign specific time frames to each section on the agenda.
- List breaks on the agenda so your audience knows what to expect.
- Allow for a few extra minutes to review the agenda.
- Always have your contact information at the bottom of the agenda.

Michael J. Lipsey

Leave a C.R.U.M. for your Memory

Remembering speeches can be a very intimidating experience, but familiarizing yourself with your presentation beforehand should be at the very core of your presentation preparation. **C.R.U.M.** is our tool for helping you memorize for your next presentation more effectively, efficiently, and expeditiously:

- **C**heat (Sheets): Otherwise known as notes. Find a format that works for you. Though some may consider 3 x 5 note cards old-fashioned, they may just be the key to unlocking the perfect presenter in you. Other options include sticky notes, an agenda printed in large type, the agenda printed on a flip chart or graphic poster, etc.

- **R**ead: There is no crime in reading material, as long as you don't read ALL of your material. Reading your notes, reading passages from books, even reading your agenda are all helpful cues to help you remember where you are, or where you need to be.

- **U**sing Visual Aids as Notes: Slides, posters, and charts are great ways to keep yourself focused, on task, and on target. Develop materials that you feel comfortable with, and begin utilizing them at once.

- **M**emorize: Commit to memory as much or all of your presentation as is humanly possible. Perhaps not word for word, but devote your major messages to memory and bridge between them with impromptu transitions that manage the flow.

5 Tips for an Effective Rehearsal

An often-overlooked process of preparing for a presentation of any size is to simply rehearse it before you give it. Whether it be in front of a mirror, in front of your boss, in front of your spouse, or on videotape, here are a few things to remember during an effective rehearsal:

- **Feedback**: Find out what you—or your rehearsal audience—found interesting, memorable, or even confusing.

- **Testing, Testing**: Test all your equipment well in advance of the presentation.

- **Visualize Your Visuals**: Rehearse using as many of the tools you plan to use during the formal presentation.

- **Rehearse Your Backup**: Don't just *have* a backup plan for if your laptop crashes or you leave your slide tray on the plane, *rehearse* it as well.

- **Use a Checklist**: Make sure that your presentation includes all of the following: Introduction, Objective, Overview, Presentation, and a Conclusion

Michael J. Lipsey

5 Easy Ways to See Yourself as Others Do

Self-perception is an intangible force we deal with on a daily basis, but what about what *others* think of you? Seeing yourself as others might is crucial to becoming a Top Performer. Here are five easy ways to help see yourself as others might:

- **Make a videotape of yourself**. Tape yourself at your next seminar or meeting or, if this is inconvenient or impractical, videotape a mock seminar or sales meeting. Then watch it, critically, several times with an objective view to what others might see and hear from you.

- **Study the tape with a friend or coach**. Outside advice is critical to seeing yourself as others do. Little things, like how many times you say "uhhm," or nervous habits you may have, like constantly running your fingers through your hair, are often invisible to you, even though they're quite obvious to others.

- **Rate yourself**. Do a self-evaluation as if you were viewing an employee, peer, or customer. Step outside of yourself and look at the salesperson standing in front of you objectively. Is he dressed professionally? Does she come off too strong? What does his office look like? These are all ways to tally up your effectiveness as a salesperson.

- **Listen to performance evaluations**. A performance evaluation from a tenant, superior, or CEO is an invaluable tool for self-constructive criticism. Everyone can improve, and if you listen carefully before denying or defending the evaluation, you will likely find ways to improve upon your performance.

- **Ask for and study feedback from customers**. Waiters and waitresses hand out comment cards after every dinner, why can't salespeople? Type up and reproduce, or simply Email, simple multiple-choice feedback forms and evaluate the ones you get back. (Not all of them will respond.)

Knowing Your Commercial Real Estate Audience

A significant part of any good presentation has to do with knowing your audience. After all, there are two halves to any good presentation: You . . . and your audience. Accordingly, this chapter deals exclusively with the various ways you and your audience interact. From eye contact to researching an audience before your presentation, you'll find invaluable tips, lists, and ideas for getting to know your audience.

8 Ways to Get to Know Your A.U.D.I.E.N.C.E.

We begin with eight simple questions to ask yourself to help you really get to know your **A.U.D.I.E.N.C.E.** These will help you give the best possible presentation, every time, for the best possible effect:

Approach: What approach will you use with this *particular* audience?

Understanding: What do you want them to understand when you're done?

Delivery: What kind of delivery would work best with *this* audience?

Inform: What can you teach them about your service, product, or company?

Eye Appeal: What visual aids will you use to better communicate your message?

Needs: What does *this* particular audience need at *this* particular time?

Compassion: How can I convey real human emotion to my audience?

Elicit Feedback: How did I do *this* time? How can I improve for *next* time?

5 Ways to Research Your Audience

It is a key step when presenting to a new group to analyze the audience beforehand. This is done through careful research using a variety of sources. Consider doing the following the next time you present to a targeted audience for the very first time:

- Interview the organization executives in charge of the event

- Review the company's Website

- Review company literature

- Research industry news via the Internet, magazines, newspapers, etc.

- Research associates within the industry

How to Present to Different Types of Audiences

Skilled presenters know that not every audience is the same. Knowing who you are presenting to—as well as *why*—is the key to successfully communicating with any group. Below are several types of audiences you will most likely come across, as well as tips on how to effectively present to them:

- **The Executives**: This type of presentation is more formal than others. Be respectful, but be knowledgeable. Just in case there are questions, always have the facts and figures to back up your recommendations. As a subordinate, you want to make sure you don't come off as lecturing to your audience or presenting yourself as "one of them." Instead, make a series of suggestions or recommended course of "actions" to your audience.

- **The Peer Group**: When presenting to a group of your industry peers, it is important that you draw them into the presentation by asking them for their opinions, experiences, and feedback. Even though you may be the expert, don't act like one with this sensitive group.

- **The Team**: The key to presenting to a team is becoming part of the team. Use words like "we" and "us," not "I" and "you." From now on, you are in a group—and it's important to make the connection with your team.

- **Mixed Groups**: Occasionally, all of the groups merge to make up one melting pot of an audience. On such occasions, it is important to structure your presentation so that within the first minutes of presenting, you are able to reach out and connect with each subgroup. Once you've put each group at ease, you can then progress with your usual presentation.

4 Questions to Ask About Your Audience

For a true analysis of your audience, look within. Knowing the various reasons *why* you are presenting to a particular audience is often just as important as knowing *how* to present in the first place. Ask yourself the following questions to determine why it is important that you speak to this particular audience:

- *Who* **is in your audience?** Are they decision-makers? Or gatekeepers? Prospects? Or current tenants? This important answer will guide the content of your material, as well as your approach in presenting it.

- *Why* **are you presenting?** Your presentation. Yourself. The two are not mutually exclusive. Why are you the one to make this presentation? Knowing what unique and special skills you bring to the podium is as important as knowing as much as you can about who is sitting in front of it.

- *What* **does your audience want?** Presenting for presenting's sake is a waste of your time, and your audience's. Knowing what your audience expects from your appearance will help you prioritize everything from your message to your visuals, and everything in between.

- *When / Where* **Is Your Presentation?** This is often the most overlooked step in the entire presentation process. Visuals, philosophies, mission statements, facts, and figures, they'll all be useless if you're too late to your presentation to prepare effectively, or the venue is not large enough for the audience. Perhaps this question should be *first* on your list, instead of last . . .

9 Ways to Motivate Your Audience

Despite their energy level—or perhaps lack of one—your audience always wants a payoff from a presentation. To provide them with one, here are nine ways to motivate your listeners:

- List three things you know will motivate your particular audience and include them in your presentation.
- If you are presenting to key decision-makers, find out how they like information presented to them.
- Intersperse your text slides with graphs, charts, and pictures.
- Give people something to do (handouts, quizzes, and discussion questions) if you are speaking for longer than half-an-hour.
- Vary the pace of your talk with some visual aids. Also, talk *without* using visuals.
- Call on the experts in the room in order to recognize their expertise.
- Include something for the visual learners, auditory learners, and audience members who like to be busy *doing* something

- For long presentations, take frequent stretch breaks rather than one long break.

Give your audience members an opportunity to talk with each other and share their views on your presentation. You can do this after you discuss each main point.

10 Ways to Use Icebreakers

An icebreaker is a vessel designed to clear a passage in frozen waters and open up channels of communications. In human terms icebreakers are intended to deal with frosty situations, cold starts, and nervous freezing. They aim not only to break ice, but also to warm the atmosphere.

Ice breakers should challenge the participants in a variety of ways—intellectual, imaginative, artistic, diplomatic, managerial, organizational—all involving communication skills. Here is a list of some simple ice breakers for you to use:

- Comment on the weather
- Make a joke
- Show a visual
- Play a video
- Do something interactive
- Ask questions
- Let them ask questions
- Perform a group activity
- Give a test
- Answer questions

6 Tips for Making Eye Contact

People speak with their eyes as well as their words. One of the best ways to make your audience feel a part of the presentation is through effective eye contact. By making eye contact with members in your audience, you will get their undivided attention and keep them interested in your presentation. Here are six great ways to do just that:

- **Alternate Sexes**: If you're wondering where to look next, why not try the old "boy, girl, boy, girl" trick. Alternating between sexes is a good way to provide a variety of eye contact for your audience.

- **The Pendulum Effect**: If a room is either predominantly male or female and the "boy, girl" trick won't work, try switching from left to right on occasion so that you don't look like you're favoring one side of the room over the other.

- **The Tennis Match**: The back of the room often gets overlooked in the challenging task of making eye contact with as many portions of the audience as possible. To avoid this mistake, try alternating the back of the room with the front of the room equally, as if watching a bouncing ball at a tennis match.

- **On the Move**: It's much easier to maintain effective eye contact with your audience when you feel comfortable enough to move out from behind the podium and approach the crowd.

- **Fanning Out**: If you're unfamiliar with the material or presenting in general, make eye contact a gradual skill by "fanning out" from one side of the room to the other. Depending on your preference, begin on the left and, slowly but surely, approach the right side of the room, making eye contact as you go.

- **Pushing Back**: A variation on the "fanning out" method, start making eye contact with the front of the room and slowly but surely move toward the back of the room. Or vice versa . . .

4 Ways to Keep Your Audience Attentive During a Video Presentation

Many a modern commercial real estate company produces a state-of-the-art promotional video to enhance sales or service presentations. Not only do these do-it-yourself segments take some of the pressure off of a presenter, but they are a nice change of pace for the audience as well. However, videos can backfire on you in more ways than one. Below are some easy tips on how to hold an audience's attention during a video:

- **Give a preview**: Tell your audience what the video is about, and why they are watching it. Setting expectations for an audience helps to keep them tuned in while they watch.

- **Make sure that your video pertains to the overall message of your presentation**. In other words, if you're presenting to existing customers, don't play the sales video, and if you're presenting to prospects, don't play the service video.

- **Edit your video**: No matter how technical, glossy, or advanced your video may seem, be sure to edit it so that it does not drag on. Only show the segments relevant to your presentation.

- **Make it a cliffhanger**: Tell your audience that the most important part of the video comes at the end. This way they'll make sure to pay close attention to the entire video so that they don't miss anything.

15 Things Your Commercial Real Estate Audience Really *Wants*

While each presenter may be different, research shows that audiences invariably call for the same things, again and again. But what are they? Where do you find these elusive requirements for connecting with every audience, every time? Right here, that's where:

Your Audience Wants You to . . . *Be prepared*
Practice. Practice. Practice. Every little bit helps!

Your Audience Wants You to . . . *Be knowledgeable*
The audience is there because they expect you to know what you are talking about . . . period!

Your Audience Wants You to . . . *Have a simple message*
You should be able to convey the meaning behind your presentation in one complete sentence. So, tell your audience what you are going to say . . .

Your Audience Wants You to . . . *Stay focused*
. . . and then *say* it. Commercial real estate groups are not interested in any filler, they want to get to the heart of the matter.

Your Audience Wants You to . . . *Give them tools they can use TODAY*
Don't just tell your audience something they *can* do, give them the tools to do it with.

Your Audience Wants You to . . . *Provide them with an agenda*

Don't keep the beginning, middle, and end of your presentation a mystery. Provide an agenda so that everyone can follow along.

Your Audience Wants You to . . . *Provide logical steps*

Don't move on until *this* step is through. Collect feedback before moving on, if necessary.

Your Audience Wants You to . . . *Recap, recap, recap*

Keep reviewing as you progress. Build these recaps into your presentation so that the flow remains clear. Recapping helps to make new material relevant and more memorable.

Your Audience Wants You to . . . *Model the behavior*

If you're sharing a tactic or trend, perform it yourself to give the audience an example of exactly what you're talking about.

Your Audience Wants You to . . . *Connect*

Ask questions of your audience, and allow them to ask questions of you. Interaction is the key to a memorable presentation.

Your Audience Wants You to . . . *Move*

Don't use the podium as a crutch. Move away from it from time to time. Don't dance, but don't just *stand* there, either.

Your Audience Wants You to . . . *Lead*

An audience may want to interact with you, but they don't want to *work*. Do the work for them by leading them where you want to go.

Your Audience Wants You to . . . *Entertain*

Stories. Anecdotes. Fables. Myths. *Gossip.* Use these entertaining tools to inform, instruct, and inspire.

Your Audience Wants You to . . . *Give concrete examples*

Use concrete examples to inform, instruct, and inspire.

Your Audience Wants You to . . . *Present to the entire group*

Don't aim too high or too low. Shoot for the middle, and everyone will follow.

Your Audience Wants You to . . . *Walk in their shoes*

Never forget that your audience has never rehearsed this speech, let alone heard the material before. It is new to them, even if you've done it a hundred times. Try to remember this if you find yourself growing impatient with their progress, or bored with the material.

10 Ways to Deal with a Hostile Audience

It happens to even the best presenters: A hostile audience ruins a great speech. But does it *have* to? Here are ten great ways to diffuse a hostile audience before they do irreparable damage to your presentation—or your *car*:

- **Repeat the question**. This age-old trick not only allows you more time to form an appropriate answer, but is the verbal equivalent of "counting to ten" before you say something rash.

- **Answer directly.** Give direct answers to direct questions. Don't try to hide your nervousness or ignorance with lies or gobbledygook. Your audience will sense this right away. If you must give an involved answer, promise to give it after your presentation to any interested parties. Most hostile audience members will lose interest by then.

- **Stay on course**. Don't allow audience hostility to throw you off course. Refer to your speech and move on.

- **Be prepared**. If you are presenting facts and figures, or controversial subject matter, be sure to back your research up with sources, statistics, facts, and figures.

- **Control your temper**. Remaining calm is the only way to avoid losing your cool. And being sarcastic or hostile back to a sarcastic or hostile audience member is one sure way to trade the audience's sympathy for you . . . to the questioner.

- **Never lie.** Always tell the truth, even if a question is difficult or unpleasant to answer. You will always get caught in a lie, always.

- **Leave your baggage at home.** Treat every audience member as an individual, and never lump all hostile audience members in with previous detractors. That's one good way to explode at a minor interruption.

- **Don't point**. Or sigh, or roll your eyes, or put your hands on your hips, etc. These are scolding poses and give you the appearance of preaching.

- **Keep momentum**. Don't allow a hostile audience to distract you from your presentation. Defer questions to after the presentation, and always, always keep moving *forward*.

- **Have a conclusion.** No matter what has happened during the presentation, always leave the audience with a well-prepared conclusion.

The Mechanics & Delivery of Presentations

Every mechanic works with nuts and bolts, and that's just what we aim to give you in this informative chapter designed to take you from Presenting A to Z.

Here you'll find tips ranging from how to set up the ideal room configuration to handling those pesky Q & As and steps to eliminating "verbal clutter." (Otherwise known as "um" and "uh.")

Presentation "Checklist"

Successful preparation prior to your presentation will enable you to devote your concentration and energy "on stage," to the delivery of the program *without* the details on your mind. Reproduce and use the following "Presentation Checklist" to assure that your mind is free to deliver your message, and not just your presentation:

Preliminary Information:

- Date _____
- Advance Publicity _____
- Time _____
- Name of Contact _____
- Location _____
- Phone Number _____
- Audience Size _____

Room Set-Up:

- Room Layout   _____
- Chairs   _____
- Lighting   _____
- Seating Plan   _____
- Tables   _____
- Electrical Outlets   _____
- Lectern   _____
- Microphone   _____

Participants' Materials:

- Manuals   _____
- Handouts   _____
- Name Cards   _____
- Supplies (pencils, paper, etc.)   _____

Visuals:

- Overhead Projector   _____
- Flip Chart   _____
- Slide Projector   _____
- VCR   _____
- Whiteboards   _____

Other Considerations:

- Clock/Timer   _____
- Start and Stop Times   _____
- Refreshments   _____
- Break and Lunch Times   _____
- Rest Room Location   _____
- Phone Area   _____
- Smoking Area   _____
- Message Location   _____

3 Types of Room Styles

The style of your venue can be just as important as your message. After all, if no one can see or hear you, how can you deliver your message in the first place? To help you decide which type of seating style is right for you, here are three of the most popular types of room styles, along with their advantages:

- **Theater style**: Best used for large audiences, this style is so-named because it resembles a theater setting. This style is easily-adjusted for larger or smaller audiences by simply adding or taking away entire aisles from the back of the room. Just remember, the larger the audience, the more careful you have to be about reaching the back of the room. Make sure your visual and audio levels are appropriate for your audience.

- **Classroom Style**: This popular style is also known as the "U-Shaped" setting. Most effective for educational and training presentations, this style works for small groups who need to be more intimate with you as a presenter.

- **Meeting Style**: This is the style you will most likely use in a day-to-day broker setting. Perfect for small groups of three to ten tenants, management teams, or sales staff, this room layout allows you to be as formal or informal as your personal style allows. You will also have a greater deal of interaction with your audience in this style.

6 Tips for Effective Room Layout

It isn't called "working the room" for nothing. The physical layout of a room affects all aspects of a successful presentation. From lighting to acoustics, from wall color to floor surfacing, it all matters, and it should all be used to your benefit. Whenever possible, you should select the room layout that works best for your personal presentation style, your message, and the services you are offering. Here are seven successful tips for making your next room layout "work" for you:

- **Preview the room:** If at all possible, visit the room personally to prepare for your presentation most effectively. If not, at least speak with the venue staff and be specific about your needs and requirements.

- **Arrive early:** If you can't preview the room, at least try to schedule your presentation so that you can get there early to make sure everything is up to snuff.

- **Check temperature:** Be sure that the room is neither too warm nor too cold to be distracting. When calculating for temperature, of course, don't go by strictly yourself. Remember to project the hundreds of warm bodies that will soon be joining you, and adjust accordingly.

- **Plan for visual aids:** Whether you use a flip-chart or slide projector, make sure there is enough room near the podium or on the stage for your equipment, and make sure there is room enough for you to maneuver around said equipment without appearing awkward.

- **Check lighting:** Be sure to check for broken overhead lighting, or ask for additional lighting if current standards are insufficient.

- **Use a Photo:** Take a photo of a room set-up that you like. When you speak with the venue staff, give them the photo to use as a guide when setting up the room. Have it on file electronically as well, in case the venue prefers Email.

- **Do better next time**: Part of an effective current presentation is planning for the future. Remembering mistakes is a great way to prepare for upcoming engagements, so always be sure to note lessons learned from past failures, such as inadequate lighting, faulty equipment, etc.

3 Ways to Stay Calm Before Presenting

Few people like to get up in front of an audience and present material to a group of strangers—or even *one* stranger. Even top performers who do it frequently still get stage fright when their name is called and the applause dies down. To get—and remain—calm before your next presentation, try the following three exercises:

- **Take a Walk:** Not just anywhere, mind you. Spend some time before your audience arrives and stroll through the venue or presentation room. Wander through the aisles, take a seat, view the podium from the back row. Putting yourself in the role of audience is sometimes all it takes to take the fear out of presenting.

- **Meet & Greet:** Don't wait until the audience has arrived, letting time tick by in some dressing room and add to your pressure. Take the fear out of the "audience" by greeting them as they enter the room. Say "hello," shake their hands, and start building "friendship" bridges. This simple action can take the mystery out of an audience and help you gain immediate impact as a presenter.

- **Breathe Deeply:** Breathing is something we all take for granted, but by concentrating on this automatic act we all engage in thousands of time a day, you can often shake those pre-presenting jitters. Close your eyes and focus on your breathing. Change the pattern of your breath and breathe deeply, then exhale. Breathe deeply, then exhale. Repeat this process several times, until your breathing is the focus—not your nerves.

10 Things to Do BEFORE a Presentation

- Smile
- Greet the first ten audience members at the door
- Wait for everyone to sit down
- Wait for everyone to *quiet* down
- Test the microphone and other equipment
- Pass out an agenda
- Make sure everyone *has* an agenda
- Provide for "sheet rustling" time
- Get a sound level on your equipment
- Greet your audience

4 Statements to Rid Yourself of Presenter's Anxiety

In ridding your anxiety over presenting, it is helpful to make definite statements about *why* you are afraid. Making these statements, and then correcting them, is one big step toward ridding yourself of presenter's anxiety altogether:

- **Tell yourself exactly *what* you are afraid of:** "I am afraid of speaking in front of an audience."

- **Explain to yourself *why* you are afraid**: "I am afraid because I think I might do something stupid and everyone will laugh at me."

- **Tell yourself why you *shouldn't* be afraid**: "I have never seen a speaker get laughed off the stage. No one has ever laughed at me during a presentation before."

- **Close with *positive thoughts* about yourself**: "I am a capable and talented person. I can give a great presentation and impress my audience."

10 Speaking Strategies of Top Performers

Speaking is more than the words coming out of your mouth. Body language, eye contact, the volume of your voice, your excitement level, and much, much more go into a good conversation, business lunch, or sales meeting. Top Performers recognize this fact, and act accordingly. The following ten strategies of Top Performers "speak" for themselves:

- Gauge the volume of your audience.

- Know your audience.

- Speak slowly and calmly, even when excited.

- Create pictures and images with your words.

- Stick with an upbeat tone.

- Focus less on being heard, and more on being *understood*.

- Your body language should reinforce your words.

- Don't use clichés, slang, or bad grammar.

- Avoid talking down to anyone.

- Speak less; listen more.

10 Mistakes Made by Presenters

When undertaking an act as challenging as making a solid presentation, people are bound to make mistakes. But knowing what to avoid is the first step in the right direction. To that end, here is a list of the top ten mistakes made by presenters:

- **No Preparation:** A presenter who isn't prepared can't hide it. Lack of preparation kills a presentation before it even lifts off. Make sure you've rehearsed your presentation, double-checked your facts, and learned from your mistakes. No one blames an inexperienced speaker, just an unprepared one.

- **Lack of Objectives:** If you don't know what your audience should do at the end of your presentation, there is no need for you to present. Knowing your objectives is the key to developing an effective presentation.

- **A Bad First Impression:** Audiences definitely judge a book by its cover, and rather quickly. Making a bad first impression, based upon your dress, your attitude, your lack of enthusiasm, or a myriad of other factors, is a good way to make a bad presentation.

- **Go Mobile:** There is nothing worse than a speaker who is glued to the floor. Move around so that your audience knows you're alive— and that you care.

- **Poor Visual Aids:** Visual aids are designed to reinforce the main points of your presentation. Without effective visuals, you are missing a key opportunity to communicate with your audience.

- **Lack of Enthusiasm:** Why should an audience be excited about your service or product, if you can't even show a little enthusiasm?

- **No Eye Contact:** Again and again, eye contact is crucial to a good presentation. No one likes—let alone trusts—a presenter who won't look them in the eye.

- **Lack of Audience Participation:** Making your presentation interactive, even if it is only with the occasional "question and answer" segment, is a serious blow to an otherwise good presentation.

- **Lack of Facial Expressions:** Effective speakers use facial expressions to help reinforce their messages. In other words, don't be a zombie. No one responds to the living dead.

- **A Weak Close:** Like closing arguments in a legal trial, the jury is always out until you make a lasting final impression. If you never do, the verdict is in: Bad Presentation. A weak close can kill a presentation.

Michael J. Lipsey

5 Common Pitfalls Made by Presenters

At times it may seem as if there are as many working parts in a solid presentation as there are in a space shuttle! By learning to avoid some of the more common errors made by inexperienced presenters, you can avoid some of those pieces-parts and "lift off" to a great and effective presentation every time:

- **Speaking Instead of *Communicating***: When you can talk to an audience of 1,000 or more as if you were talking to a close friend, you have learned the final hurdle of presenting: Good presenters don't speak, they communicate. Communicating means sharing your ideas honestly and intelligently with a receptive audience who understands them. "Did the audience get it?" That is the kind of question you should be asking yourself after every presentation. Not, "Did they like me?" or "Will they buy?"

- **An Expert Hangover**: You probably learned—way back in high school—that statistics, passages, and quotes are great to use in a presentation. While this is worthy advice, many overworked and underpaid presenters simply string together all of the above, ad nauseum, until there is very little substance to their presentation. Avoid using the quick way out. If you're considering using too much filler, why not also consider simply shortening your presentation?

- **An Audience Out of Control**: While most audiences are professional and respectful, any presenter can lose control of her audience if she allows for too many interruptions or questions at one time. Handle interruptions quickly and professionally, and then move on just as quickly. Audiences expect to be led by a good presenter, so it is your job to lead them accordingly.

- **Admitting Ignorance**: Ignorance has gotten a bad rap. Strictly defined, the word *ignorance* simply means "a lack of knowledge." Lacking knowledge is not a bad thing, if you strive to acquire it as efficiently as possible. When someone asks you a question that you don't know, admit that you don't know the answer, and then try to find out. During the break, make a few calls or search the Web. Returning with a straight answer is a lot more legitimate than bluffing in the first place, and then getting caught!

- **Wrapping Up:** Many presenters don't really warm up until their presentation is over; and then they don't want to stop. Adding on layers and layers of information as your presentation is over is a sure way to lose your audience, and waste your time and effort. Design your presentation with a clear beginning, middle, and end, then stick to it as you speak. Spreading your information out over the entire presentation is more effective than piling it on at the end.

Michael J. Lipsey

7 Tips for Using Your Voice Effectively

There are many things you simply can't control during a presentation. How much sleep your audience members got the night before. The color of the walls. The parking at the venue. Even today's modern technology makes controlling the air conditioning occasionally impossible.

Yet of all the physical elements you *can* control during a presentation, the tone, sound, and quality of your voice rests at, or at least very near, the top of the list. Here are seven great ways you can use your voice more effectively during your next presentation:

- **Adjust your own volume:** While it is occasionally annoying when a speaker talks too loud, nothing is worse than having to strain to hear a speaker present. Practice several times in a large venue to get the volume of your voice just right.

- **Don't speak in a monotone voice:** Nothing puts an audience to sleep more quickly than speaking in the same voice for the duration of your speech.

- **Alternate the tone of your voice:** To avoid sounding monotone, vary your speech patterns. For instance, you should use a different voice for personal anecdotes than you do for presenting dry facts and figures. Practice this first, or you may sound unprepared or flustered.

- **Slow it down occasionally:** When key points arise in your presentation, it is best to slow down. This way, you can verbally emphasize to your audience that what you are saying is important.

- **Pause for effect:** Since it happens too rarely in a presentation, silence is an excellent exclamation point. By slightly extending a pause, you can add emphasis and importance to the key points in your presentation.

- **Drink:** Remember to take a drink before your next presentation. Water or your favorite beverage of choice will prevent potential voice problems during your presentation.

- **When in doubt, steal:** If you're struggling to find your own voice and lacking inspiration, why not watch the national or even local news. Professional news anchors provide some of the best examples of effective voice usage on the market today.

6 Ways to E.S.C.A.P.E. the Ordinary Presentation

Audiences, especially potential tenants, are eager to **E.S.C.A.P.E.** the ordinary sales call or seminar with a presenter who takes them away from the everyday speech they've already seen before. When asked about the personal characteristics that best describe the "perfect" presenter, audiences say they want a presenter who is:

- **Enthusiastic:** Show your audience that you are more than happy to be there by positive mannerisms, words, and expressions.

- **Sincere:** Don't schmooze your audience. Be believable through your words and actions.

- **Confident:** Don't simply memorize your service stats or fascinating figures. Instead: *Know* your topic. Only by being fluent and familiar with what you have to offer will you ever be truly convincing.

- **Articulate:** Learning to speak slowly or confidently is a tool, not the ends to the means. What you say is more important than how you say it. Choose your words carefully and never stop learning the best words to use.

- **Passionate:** How many lackluster speakers convinced you to be excited about their service? Do you remember what they said? In order to be memorable, you *must* be passionate!

- **Energetic:** Audiences love speakers who aren't glued to the podium, eyes down on their prepared speech. Be yourself but, most importantly, enjoy yourself! Wow your audience with your own sense of style and delivery.

10 Things to Do DURING a Presentation

- Show enthusiasm
- Make eye contact
- Refer to your agenda
- Recap when appropriate
- Provide adequate time for breaks
- Answer questions promptly and professionally
- Vary your voice levels for impact
- Work the audience
- Use checklist for items needed to be covered
- Make a strong close

6 Tips for Keeping Your Listing/Sales Presentation Interesting

No matter how many times you present, there are always ways to make your next one better. Sometimes, presenting too often can actually be a liability instead of an asset. After all, when you make frequent presentations, how in the world do you ever manage to keep them interesting? Here are six quick tips for doing just that:

- **Eye Appeal:** No matter how well you speak, your audience invariably wants you to show them what you are talking about—literally. Depending on your preference, use color graphics, slides, and handouts to get your message across. Effective visuals such as these will help to communicate your main points, and keep your audience fully engaged.

- **Step Away From the Podium**: Many speakers use the podium as a security blanket, whether consciously or subconsciously. Don't get stuck in this trap. Get out in front of your audience and interact with them. You'll find *more* freedom in front of the podium, not less.

- **Make Eye Contact**: Make sure you always maintain eye contact with your audience. Many speakers translate this to mean "staring," but as a rule you should make eye contact with an audience member for three to five seconds at a time. Then move on. You should also vary where it is you are looking, making sure to make eye contact with all areas of the room, including those seats in the back.

- **Focus on Your Audience**: Visual aids, or "visuals," are designed to provide your audience with visual reinforcements of your verbal message. Use them as such, and not merely as a crutch when you run out of words.

- **Be Yourself**: Never try to be something you aren't. Audiences can smell a fake quicker than a free lunch. Develop your own presentation style and use it! If you're not a gymnast, don't do cartwheels. Convey your positivity in a manner that's more natural for you.

- **NEVER Give a** *Speech*: A speech is something an audience hates instinctively, and nothing says "speech" like staring straight down at the podium as you read your notes. Notes are fine, as a reference, as a tool, but never as a means to an end.

4 Steps to a More Dynamic Delivery

There are four integral steps to the proper delivery of a winning sales presentation. They include the "Warm Up," "Presenting Solutions/Features and Benefits to Decision Makers," the "Trial Close," and the "Close." What follows is a brief explanation of each:

Step 1: Warm Up

- Establish a connection with your audience with a story, humor, or current news.

- Don't say, "I want to thank you for letting me speak to you..." This will make you sound just like everyone else making a presentation. Your goal is to stand apart from them and sell your idea.

- Don't sit. Standing creates a greater sense of authority.

- Look them in the eye and use their names.

Step 2: Presenting Features and Benefits to Decision Makers

- Remember, you are selling an idea or thing to a person or group of people. Tell them something about what you are selling (*feature*); then immediately tell them how it will fulfill a need for them (*benefit*).

- The needs analysis and the agenda have made it obvious which issues they are.

- Use visuals to overcome objections or to reinforce benefits. Visual aids should support your points, not the other way around. Talk to your audience rather than at your slides.

- Don't overdo the visuals *or* the technology. They should support the case; the technology should not be the only part of the presentation that is remembered.

Step 3: Trial Close

- Ask questions, such as, "What do you think? Or "Does this solve the problem?"
- If they say, "yes," go directly to step 4, The Close.
- If there are questions or objections, listen to what is being asked. Paraphrase the question to make sure that you understand the problem and ensure that everyone hears the question.
- If the question is still holding things hostage, Negotiate/Brainstorm a solution.

Step 4: Close

- **Summary Close**: Summarize all the needs that have been met and ask for permission/sale.
- **Urgency Close**: This is time sensitive (the price will go up, the competition will get it tomorrow, etc.)
- **Other Closing Techniques**: Chain, Sharp Angle, Smoke Out, Minor Point, Alternate Choice, Instruction Close.
- If your close is rebuffed, ask questions to find out the objection.

15 Steps to a Powerful Presentation

- Rapport
- Agenda
- Bring Your Case
- Trail Close
- Handle Questions
- Acknowledge Those in your Company that Serve the Tenant
- Stay Ahead of the Assignment
- Do Whatever it Takes to get your Company to Honor Your Promises
- Understand The Approval Process
- Always have a Creative Solution that will improve their business
- Use their Mission Statement
- Have Major Proposals Reviewed by Peers
- Demonstrate how you would use Teams
- Continuous Feedback
- Close when Appropriate

5 Bad Delivery Habits

So you write a great presentation and design state-of-the-art visual aids. Then, you stand up in front of the audience and lose them in ten minutes—simply because of bad delivery habits. Worst of all, you don't even know what you are doing that is so distracting. Below are some common delivery pitfalls and how to avoid them.

- **Clothing**: Always dress appropriately. When researching your audience, find out what the dress code for the day is and dress accordingly.

- **Turning your back**: Practice using your preferred methods of visual aids so that you don't have to turn your back to use them.

- **Typos**: Take care to edit your slides, agendas, and handouts, then edit them some more. Misspelled words signify sloppiness and cost credibility.

- **Using too many filler words:** Useless words such as "uh," "and," "um," and "you know," are used to fill dead air space. More importantly, they distract your audience, decrease the effectiveness of your presentation, and diminish your authority as a speaker.

- **Too many gestures:** The only thing worse than using no gestures at all during a presentation is using too *many* gestures.

5 Ways to Eliminate Filler Words

Top Performers often have to master skills that baffle the rest of the population, such as removing filler words such as "uh" and "um" from their presentations, a feat which few of us ever successfully master. Here are five ways to eliminate filler words from your next presentation:

- **Work on Your Transitions**: Studies show that transitions are the most common pitfall for filler words such as "um" and "uh." Therefore, working on your transitions from one topic to the next should help eliminate these unpleasant and distracting phrases. Some more attractive transition phrases might be "moving on," "next," or "finally."

- **The Pause That Refreshes**: There's an old saying that goes, "If you can't say something nice, don't say anything at all." Work on silence instead of fillers. As you feel yourself getting ready to spout yet another "um" or "uh," try simply not saying anything. It works.

- **Substitute Behaviors**: Sometimes what you *do* can replace what you *say*. If filler words are a problem for you, why not try a behavior to eliminate them, such as smiling every time you feel the urge to say, "umm." However, it's important not to substitute a filler *behavior* for a filler word!

- **The Phrase that "Pays"**: If transitions are where those pesky filler words pop up, inserting a "phrase that pays" may be just the ticket. Phrases that pay might be something like "now, for our next section," or "if you'll follow me," or perhaps something of your own choosing.

- **Practice Makes Perfect**: The best way to avoid filler words is simply to practice, practice, practice. Filler words are the brain's way of saying, "what now?" When you ALWAYS know what's coming next, you eliminate the need for filler words altogether.

5 Barriers to Effective Communication

Let's face it: Giving a presentation is *never* easy. But in your haste to give a good presentation, don't overlook the very reason for a presentation in the first place: the audience. Being properly dressed and well prepared with the latest research and visuals is one thing, turning off an audience with one of the following Five Barriers to Communication is quite another thing. A *bad* thing:

- **Defying Definitions**: No one denies that commercial real estate is a business with its own unique dictionary of terms and words. But as you try to stay on the cutting edge, avoid talking down to your audience by leaving them in the dark about your "big words." If you do define a new concept, it is only fair—not to mention smart—that you take time out to define it before continuing.

- **Clichés**: No one enjoys tired clichés, except perhaps for bumper sticker companies. Pandering to your audience with such bumper sticker statements—your attitude determines your altitude, you can't spell success without "u," et al—tends to have the same effect as elevator music: Drowsiness!

- **Pretentiousness**: Remember that as a presenter it is your job to inform, not to impress! Avoid creating communication barriers by using formal or "big" words. These inflated words often make you appear less credible than you may well be. Remember, keeping it simple is usually the best approach.

- **Preaching**: It's hard not to be enthusiastic about a service, property, or product, but avoid being preachy at all costs. Your presentation should be no longer, or shorter, than it has to be, and if you find yourself going on and on, you might want to consider chopping off five minutes so that your prospects get the main ideas, not everything but the kitchen sink.

- **Technical Jargon**: Speaking to a group of targeted prospects like those in your chosen field should eliminate the use of technical jargon whatsoever. You all know what you're doing, so why take time using five-dollar words to explain it?

4 Ways NOT To Go Blank During Your Presentation!

It's happened to every presenter at times, even the top of the Top Performers: You're in a groove, speaking your heart out, the audience is eating out of your hands and then, suddenly, you lose your train of thought! Panic sets in, sweat starts to bead on your forehead, now what? Relax. With the following four tips, you may still go blank, but at least you'll be prepared when it happens:

- **Always have notes:** Even if you've given your presentation a hundred times, bring notes. A sheet of paper listing your main topics is usually all that you'll need, and you can quickly scan down the list to see where you were headed.

- **Ask questions:** When your mind really does go blank, buy yourself a little extra time—while still not losing momentum—by asking a question or two that relates to either what you were talking about, or your company, service, or products in general. While the audience is busy forming an answer to your question, you'll find your focus all over again and can soon move on without incident.

- **Have a short anecdote ready:** If all else fails, prepare a short, quick anecdotal story that has to do with your area of expertise. Chances are, by the time the story is done, you'll be back on track.

- **Have an agenda:** Last but not least, direct your audience to look through their agenda while you do as well. This short breather will help redirect your audience, and yourself, to the next point.

Michael J. Lipsey

10 Things NOT to do When Making a Presentation

It's often just as helpful to know what NOT to do as to know how to do something. Such is the case with the following ten things to NOT do when giving a presentation:

- Try to fool the audience.
- Talk down to the audience.
- Read it straight from your text.
- Schmooze the audience.
- Use inside office jokes.
- Laugh at your own jokes.
- Make your audience the butt of a joke.
- Provide printed material with errors on it.
- Go too long without breaks.
- Exceed the time limit.

5 Ways to Gesture Effectively

Gestures are reflections of every speaker's individual personality. What's right for one speaker may not be right for another; however, the following five rules apply to anyone who seeks to become an effective speaker:

- **Be Natural:** The most effective gesture will be the most effective gesture for *you*. A gesture that looked cool on someone else may not play well for you, and vice versa. Chances are, the gestures you are currently using are what are already comfortable for you.

- **Be Practical:** It's not always practical to use too many gestures, but it's never practical to use *none*. Deciding to use gestures is as important as deciding which gestures to use.

- **Be Choosy:** Don't have a repertoire of thirty gestures, choose three. Be they the "time-out" gesture or the finger quotation marks, being selective about your gestures could just mean the difference between looking energetic, and spastic.

- **Be Appropriate:** Some gestures "play big," others don't. For instance, when speaking to a large audience, your gestures will be bigger, broader so that those in the back of the room can see them. This doesn't play well in a smaller, more intimate setting, where your gestures should be more close to the vest and reserved.

- **Be Consistent:** Whichever gestures you choose, make them consistent. The more you use a gesture, the more smooth and practiced it becomes. It also becomes ingrained in your "pattern" of gestures, and will look less awkward or rehearsed.

Preparing for the Dreaded Q & A Session

Many of today's presentations don't end with a grand finale, they slowly build up to an appropriate, informative, and professional Question and Answer session, otherwise known as the Q & A. Here is how to best prepare for the dreaded Q & A:

- The best way to prepare yourself and build your confidence is to take the time to write down as many possible questions as you can think of, and then practice answering them prior to the event.

- To get more ideas of possible questions, you can ask others to pose questions to you and practice answering them.

- It is particularly important to practice answering what you consider the most difficult questions. Then, if you do get that question, or a similar one, you will be better prepared to respond than if you were totally unprepared.

- Unless you are dealing with a very hostile audience, most questions are much easier than you anticipate they will be. If you are prepared to answer the most difficult questions you can think of, handling the less difficult ones will be easy to do.

- While a question and answer session can be stressful, it can also offer you an opportunity to clarify things your audience may not have understood or repeat things you think are important.

Handling the Dreaded Q & A

While many presenters dread this situation, most see it as an opportunity to cover those points they might have missed due to lack of time or preparation, and for audience members to clarify parts they might have missed. Below are several great steps for how to handle the Q & A:

- **Listen to the entire question:** Too many people start responding to a question before the entire question is even asked. Not waiting to hear the entire question can result in you providing a response that had nothing to do with the question. Force yourself to LISTEN to the entire question and make sure you understand it.

- **Pause before answering:** Allow yourself time to value the question and listener. REPEAT the question out loud so the entire audience can hear it. It is important that everyone "hear" the question, or the answer you provide may not make sense to some of the people.

- **Give credit:** You may say something like, "That was a great question" or, "Glad you asked that question," or even, "I get asked that question by many people." One word of caution: If you credit one person with asking a question, be sure to credit EVERYONE for asking a question. You don't want people to feel their question was not as important.

- **Respond to the Question** as honestly as you can. If you don't know an answer to a question, do not try to fake it. Be honest, and tell them you do not know but promise to research the answer for them and DO get back to them.

- **Bridge** to the next question by asking a question. "Does that answer your question?" "Is that the kind of information you were looking for?" Etc. Once they respond to you in the affirmative, you now have permission to go onto the next person.

- **Ask** people to stand up when they ask a question. This does two things: (1) It shows you who is asking the question, and (2) It makes it easier for the audience to also hear the question.

- **Have** small sheets of paper available for people to write down their questions during your presentation. They may forget what they were going to ask earlier.

- **Allow** people to pass the questions to you if they feel uncomfortable standing up and asking the question out loud. This gives the person who truly wants to ask a question an option.

- **Always** repeat the question. This does three things: (1) It makes sure you understood the question, (2) It gives you a chance to value the question and think of an answer, and (3) It assures the other people in the audience can hear the question, since you are facing them.

- **Always** take time to think "before" you answer all questions. This allows you time to think, especially for those difficult questions. Do the same for those questions you readily know the answer for. Responding too quickly to those questions you are most comfortable with will only bring attention to those questions you do not.

- **Have** a pencil and paper available for you to write down questions you can't answer. You may even elect someone to record the questions on paper. This way, you can properly follow up with the person who asked the question you couldn't answer. Be sure to get their name and phone number or address. Promise to get back to them and DO get back to them.

15 Rules for Handling Questions

Questions will inevitably come up during your presentation, and you should be prepared to answer them to the best of your ability. Some questions will be easier than others, and vice versa. Here are fifteen hard and fast rules for more effective ways to handle questions during your very next presentation:

- If time allows, the best time to take questions is at any time *during* your presentation. If time is an issue, ask for questions *before* your summary.

- Make sure you fully understand the question before you begin to answer.

- Repeat a question to the entire audience if you believe that they may not have heard the question.

- When responding to a question, begin by looking at the person who asked it. However, don't continue looking at that person if the answer is fairly long.

- Always answer the question to the group.

- Once you have finished answering the question, it may be appropriate to return to the questioner and ask, "Does that answer your question?"

- Keep your voice comfortable and friendly, even in tough situations.

- Some people ask multiple questions, or combine two separate issues within a single question. Deal with each point individually.

- Avoid letting people monopolize too much of your presentation time with their "opinion."

- If all else fails, it is acceptable for you to ask them to meet with you after the presentation to discuss the issue.

- It's acceptable to say, "I don't know." It is much better to admit to not knowing rather than "faking your way through an answer."

- Use visuals to help answer questions if they are available from your presentation.

- Be prepared to promise that you will look into the concern further and get back to the person with the answer.

- If appropriate, ask the audience for help in answering the question.

- Apply four basic steps when answering questions: **Listen, Support, Answer,** and **Follow Up**.

3 Ways to Handle Objections More Effectively

Be prepared to handle objections. Throughout your presentation, the tenant(s) will express acceptance or rejection in varying degrees. Don't be discouraged by objections. An objection is really an opportunity for you to better align yourself with your customer's real—and often unspoken—needs.

Think of objections as neutral or positive signs that mean the customer is paying attention and is actually considering your proposal. In general, "Dealing with Objections" has three steps:

- **Clarify:** Probe for the source of the objection. An objection is ultimately rooted in a basic need that you have not met—yet.

- **Act:** Build a response that directly addresses the source need.

- **Confirm:** Check to see that the prospect has accepted and is ready to move on.

3 Steps to a More Effective Closing

Closing a sale is the natural and logical outcome of an effective presentation. Ask for agreement and action. Asking for agreement always puts some pressure on the customer to make a decision. The amount of pressure you should risk creating depends on where you are in the process, how many benefits the customer has accepted, and the quality of trust and rapport you have established.

Once you have delivered your Close, you should reaffirm the customer's positive decision. The customer has just made a major decision; it is natural to have doubts.

Communicate that your concern goes beyond closing the deal— that this is just the beginning of your "relationship" with your new customer. Ensure the customer that you will follow up and make sure the product/service continues to meet the customer's needs and expectations.

- **Be concise**: Make each word count. Avoid unnecessary statements that could be misinterpreted.

- **Close with confidence**: Act as if you expect the customer to accept your proposal and do not convey uncertainty.

- **Establish eye contact**: Ask, in a friendly way, for the commitment.

10 Great Ways to "Conclude with Conviction"

All good things must come to an end, but when you "conclude with conviction," chances are you are just *beginning*—a healthy sales relationship with the prospect, that is. Here are ten great ways to close with conviction.

- Save time for your conclusion so you don't have to rush through it.

- Let your audience know you are about to conclude with statements such as "Finally, or "In conclusion . . ."

- Don't read your conclusion. End by looking straight at your audience.

- Keep your voice confident and strong for the duration of the conclusion.

- Make your conclusion brief and to the point, and then **stop**.

- Summarize clearly the key areas you covered. (Recap!)

- Recommend specific action steps during your conclusion.

- Find some convincing statistics to use as you conclude.

- Review using a picture of what you want people to keep in their minds.

- Reinforce the benefits of doing what you recommend.

10 Things to Do AFTER a Listing/Sales Presentation

- Smile
- Provide a **verbal** summary of the points you covered
- Provide a **printed** summary of the points you covered
- Thank your audience
- Open the floor to questions
- Make any additional handouts and materials available
- Make yourself available
- Provide the audience with a method of reaching you
- Get feedback
- Apply feedback to your next presentation

30 Questions for Evaluating Your Presentation

Feedback is an important tool for your ongoing growth as an effective presenter. If possible, videotape or at least tape-record your next presentation, or even your next *rehearsal* for your next presentation. If not, have a colleague, spouse, or friend observe one. Then ask yourself, or them, the following thirty questions to assess your latest presentation, and improve for your next one:

- Was the speech well organized?
- Did the organization support the purpose of the presentation?
- Did the structure hold the audience's attention?
- Were concrete examples used to support the speech?
- Did the speech flow logically and smoothly?
- Did I use interesting facts and figures?
- Did the speech relate directly to the purpose?
- Was the subject appropriate to the audience?
- Did I hold the audience's attention?
- How did the audience respond to the speech?
- Did I say something meaningful and valuable?
- Have I made a contribution to the audience's thinking?
- Was any humor I may have used well received?
- Was original or new material presented?
- Did my overall appearance support my purpose?
- Did my body language match my words?
- Did I use vocal variety?
- Did my voice support my actions?
- Could everyone hear me?

- Was my voice used for emphasis?
- Was I enthusiastic about the subject?
- Did I appear confident?
- Did I show an interest in the audience?
- Did I use appropriate language for this particular audience?
- Did the language support my purpose?
- Did I choose power words?
- Were the words *pronounced* correctly?
- Were the words *used* correctly?
- How effective was the use of my words?
- How did the speech make the audience *feel*?

Other Opportunities to Present

Not all presentations take place in a large meeting hall or intimate conference room. How many of us have found ourselves faced with the opportunity for a quick, abbreviated, impromptu presentation at an everyday place, such as the store?

How to Present . . . at a Party

Another great place to provide a quick, impromptu presentation is at a party. Here's how:

- If you find yourself standing alone in a corner of the room, don't just eat all the spinach dip: Initiate a conversation with the next person who walks by.
- Introduce yourself to two new people.
- Participate in a group discussion, but do not dominate the conversation.
- Have a conversation with someone you may have not seen in a while.
- When they respond, ask for a few minutes of their time. When they grant them, and most people will, give an abbreviated version of your presentation.
- Always follow up the presentation with your business card. Also, ask for theirs.

How to Present . . . in an Elevator

Hold that door. Going up? Another great place to provide a quick, impromptu presentation is in an elevator. Here's how:

- Initiate a friendly greeting.

- Ask them how their day is going.

- When they answer, ask for a few minutes of their time. When they grant them, and most people will, give an abbreviated version of your presentation.

- Always follow up the presentation with your business card. Also, ask for theirs.

How to Present . . . at the Airport

Ever been stranded at the airport, waiting several hours for your latest layover to end? Here's how turn a liability into an asset while presenting at the airport:

- Find some way to initiate the conversation, be it a comment on the weather or a request for the time.

- Ask the person where they are going. Is it for business or pleasure?

- If it's for business, ask what business they're in. Now ask how long have they been delayed?

- When they answer, ask for a few minutes of their time. When they grant them, and most people will, give an abbreviated version of your presentation.

- Always follow up the presentation with your business card. Also, ask for theirs.

Presentation Tools: *Visual Aids*

Modern technology and sophisticated audiences have given rise to a new breed of visual aids. Glitzy, glossy, sleek, and agile, these techno tools are as numerous as they are sophisticated. So what can you do to stay on top of the visual aid dilemma? The best rule of thumb is to attend as many presentations as you can. See who is using what and when and how.

Then let your personality be your guide. If you are not comfortable with techno gadgets and bells and whistles, begin adding technology slowly to your presenter's arsenal. Don't over- or under-present—by now you should have researched your audience. If a simple flip chart and slide show will work, why spend extra time, money, and resources on the technological equivalent?

After all, from Power Point to laser pointers, chances are today's technology will soon be eclipsed by tomorrow's. For this reason, our section on visual aids will deal with the practice of using visual aids, and not the tools themselves.

5 Reasons Why You Should Use Visual Aids

Why use visuals? Visual aids can be powerful tools for beefing up an already effective presentation. Specifically, they have five important benefits:

- **They increase understanding**: Effective visual aids, such as helpful charts, graphs, or illustrations, help to convey messages clearly.

- **They save time**: Ever heard the saying, "A picture is worth a thousand words?"

- **They enhance retention**: When your audience can both see AND hear your message, you double your effectiveness.

- **They promote attentiveness**: Visuals help keep your audience focused on your message—not just your words.

- **They help control nervousness**: Displaying visual aids gives you something to do. This "purposeful activity" uses up nervous energy without distracting the audience

5 Common Forms of Visual Aids

Whatever mode you chose for your visual aid, if you chose to use data, use graphic presentations rather than tabular material; a graph with a strong diagonal line depicting growth is far more persuasive than a list of percentages. The five Visual Aid methods most often used are:

- **Video Tape**: A good video will spur the viewers into action. It should last between three to six minutes, have a strong introduction with music, images, brief interview with management and success stories from satisfied tenants. (See "How to Handle a Video Presentation" for tips.)

- **Slide Presentation**: This can make a great impression. During your three to six minute presentation, introduce your tenant pictorially to your product, show graphs or charts that visually reflect high customer satisfaction and favorable competitive comparisons. A well organized, properly targeted collection of slides can keep your presentation on track and on schedule.

- **Overhead Transparencies**: This is an inexpensive but effective way to deliver information. An important testimonial letter can be copied onto a transparency for little more than the cost of a photocopy. Likewise, you can put copies of your new ad campaign, display a new copy of a recent order placed by a large competitor. Because you can write on a blank transparency with dry marker, you can spontaneously illustrate a cost analysis or clarify a certain point in front of the entire group.

- **Handouts, Flipcharts, Models, and Blackboards** . . . can all be used to enhance and support your presentation. The visual information you present will be more memorable to your audience.

- **PowerPoint**: This form of presenting incorporates both text and graphical analysis and is very ideal when presenting to large groups. It is important to consider the background and text colors selected to create your presentation. Color will affect how the audience perceives what you are presenting.

10 Types of Visual Aids

There are many different types of visual aids, from laser pointers to the reliable slide show. The types of visual aids most commonly used include:

- Props
- Models
- White boards
- Chalkboards
- Charts
- Posters
- Flip charts
- Overhead transparencies
- Old-fashioned slides
- Computer projection slides

10 Criterion for Choosing Visual Aids

Effective visual aids range from flip charts to expensive multi-media extravaganzas such as PowerPoint. Your choice for a particular presentation depends on the following various factors:

- The information you want to convey
- How you want to convey it
- Your comfort level with various technologies
- The size of your audience
- The physical environment of the room
- The technology available
- The equipment available to you
- The training available
- The time available to prepare visuals
- The amount of money you can afford

6 Tips for Effective Visuals

Today's savvy modern audiences are high on expectations and low on attention spans. Not only do they demand dynamic speakers, but they've been trained by television and the movies to expect to "see" something. To meet this excessive demand, it is imperative to use the best visual aids at your disposal. To help you in that quest, here are some great tips for the most effective visuals:

- **Think billboard:** The best test for your visuals is the "billboard test." If you were looking at it while passing in a car, would it make sense? If not, redesign it until it does.

- **Test Your Visuals**: Are they easy to read? Do they illustrate your point? Are they simple to follow?

- **Bullet Points Only**: Full, complete sentences are too long and too busy for visual displays.

- **Use Color Sparingly**: A good rule of thumb is to use two colors in your graphics. More than three will make your visual too busy.

- **Less is More:** As a general rule, there should be no more than 20 words of text per visual.

- **Keeping it real:** If available, the actual samples of your products are the best visual aid available. Selling a service? Why not tie in a related tactile aid, such as giveaway key chains for your next property, etc.

15 Tips for Designing Effective Visual Aids

- Title each screen
- Use larger fonts and perhaps different style/colors for titles
- Use one visual to illustrate one point
- Make diagrams simple and accurate
- Keep visuals simple
- Stick to one size
- Stick to one style
- Stick to one font
- All screens must be stand-alone
- No more than six bullet points per slide
- Use graphics symbols where possible to show ideas
- Use pie charts for comparison of components
- Use line charts to show trends
- Order points by order of importance
- When possible, combine sound, image, and motion

Using Visual Aids as Notes

Memorization is a virtual impossibility for long presentations, reading from a script an unattractive alternative for short ones. So why not use your visual aids—as notes? Using your slides, computer monitors, transparencies, or flip chart pads as notes has four important advantages:

- **What comes next?** Your next visual aid has your next major idea on it. Use effective titles that properly capture the main message of the visual aid.

- **Feel free to move around the room**: Movement helps you to relax and adds energy to your presentations. Movement also allows your audience to follow you and pay closer attention to you.

- **Maintain eye contact**: You can look at your audience all the time, except when you look briefly at your visual aid.

- **Boost your audience confidence level**: Well-designed visual aids show that you have a plan and are following it. This gives your audience unspoken confidence in your abilities as a seasoned presenter.

6 More Ways to Use Notes

You need to feel comfortable with whatever form of notes you prefer to use. Here are some additional guidelines when using notes:

- Use as few notes as possible. In fact, if you can get away from using notes, it's recommended that you do so.

- Keep your notes simple. Stick with an outline that has main points, key words or phrases.

- Use your notes only as a reference guide to keep you on track and help you be sure that you don't forget any key ideas.

- Place your notes on a lectern or on a table in front of you, or to your side. Try not to hold them.

- Try not to "read" your notes. It gives the appearance that you are unprepared.

- Write notes in the borders of flip charts or transparencies in a way that only you can see them.

Michael J. Lipsey

10 Tips for Using Computer Presentations

Modern technology has brought us into the computer age, and many speakers prefer to use computer generated presentations, such as PowerPoint, as opposed to so-called "old-fashioned" tools such as slide shows and flip-charts. For those brave souls, here are a few tips on using computer presentations:

- **Use LARGE fonts.** Small fonts are hard to read.

- **Use contrasting colors.** A dark background with light text is easily readable.

- **Use drop shadows.** Adding drop shadows to text makes it more legible.

- **Keep the background simple.** Too much going on in the background is distracting.

- **Avoid using red or yellow text.** These colors are often hard to read.

- **AVOID ALL CAPS!** It will seem like you're shouting.

- **Variety is the key.** Include a good combination of words, pictures, and graphics.

- **Turn up the volume.** Incorporate sound effects or audio clips into presentations.

- **Don't rely on the Internet.** Use pre-stored graphics to avoid being delayed by too slow or unreliable web connections.

- **Stay current.** Technology is always advancing. Subscribe to a business/technology magazine to stay current on the latest tips to make your job easier.

Using Color in Multimedia Presentations

Does it *really* matter what background color to use in a presentation? Is there a certain color that communicates authority? What about a color that evokes loyalty? The answers are yes, yes, and yes. The colors for type, illustrations, and backgrounds influence the way they are perceived. Here is a basic guide to using color in your presentations.

- **Red:** excitement, alert
- **Green:** growth
- **Yellow:** confidence, warmth, wisdom
- **Purple:** dignity, sophistication
- **White:** professionalism, new, innocence
- **Blue:** truth, trust, justice
- **Black:** authority, strength
- **Orange:** action, optimism
- **Brown:** friendliness, warmth
- **Gray:** integrity, maturity

Michael J. Lipsey

Advantages and Disadvantages of Overhead Transparencies

Just low-tech enough to soothe the technologically challenged, but mechanical enough to feel like you're putting on a show, overhead transparencies have always been a popular presenter's tool. But are they right for you? Below are advantages and disadvantages of using overhead transparencies.

Advantages

- Inexpensive
- Easy to use
- Easy to *see*
- Wide availability
- Relatively low-tech, but still impressive

Disadvantages

- Unwieldy
- Transparencies are fragile
- Usually black and white
- Changing transparencies can be awkward
- They can be noisy

14 Tips for Using Flip Charts in Your Next Sales/Listing Presentation

There is an art to using flip charts, and we're not talking about your handwriting! To an awkward or nervous presenter, adding the factor of a flip chart could spell disaster if she comes unprepared. Flip charts may seem low-tech, but for the smaller, more intimate presentations you're likely to make on a day-to-day basis, they may just fit the bill. With proper planning and a little bit of work, you can turn an average flipchart into a dynamic, high-quality visual aid. Here's how:

- **Key Points Only.** If you put too many thoughts or ideas on the page, you run the risk of losing the audience's focus.

- **No More Than 6 Lines of Text**. Don't crowd the page with words. Keep your audience focused on the important points.

- **Bullets & Lists**. Help your audience separate main ideas by using bullets in list form.

- **Color to Highlight.** Consider alternating between two colors so the audience can tell where a new idea begins and ends. Avoid using too *many* colors. Choose one dark color and one accent color, such as blue and red or green and brown, and stick with them for all sheets of the pad. Never use pink, orange, or yellow markers. They are impossible to see and make your audience strain their eyes.

- **Plenty of Blank Space.** White space on the flipchart enables an audience to better focus on key points.

- **Bring your own markers.** Never assume the venue has markers for you, or a business center in case you forget to bring your own. Instead, plan ahead and bring a set of color markers with you.

- **Find a flip chart stand that is convenient, portable, and low maintenance**. The fancy, more expensive models often require an engineering degree to put together, and you want something lightweight and portable that sets up in a breeze once you're at the presentation venue. Make sure the flip charts you use match the stand you prefer. Mix and match both styles until you find a fit that's perfect for quick setup, convenient transport, and strong security.

- **Choose your flip chart pads as carefully as you choose your stand**. Go with lined over plain, to help you keep lettering straight and not slanted. Also, choose pads with individual sheets that are perforated at the top, so that you're not tearing off raggedy edges in a pinch.

- **Sketch particular charts ahead of time** before you translate them onto the big pad.

- **To increase neatness, lightly write your text in pencil** first before using markers.

- **NEVER use ALL CAPS.** They have the same effect as SHOUTING! Using upper and lower case letters makes your message easier to read.

- **To prevent "ghosting,"** or material from other pages from peeking through, have a blank sheet of paper between each page of your pad.

- **Invest in a case**, even if it's made out of cardboard, in order to properly store and transport your flip charts.

- **Recycle your flip charts.** If you're giving the same presentation to several groups a month, there's no need to reinvent the wheel. As long as you take care with the chart the first time, it should be good for at least a month or two.

Advantages and Disadvantages of Flip Charts

Every visual aid has its pros and cons. Flip charts are no exception. These lightweight and portable presentation materials are loved by many, scorned by an equal number. Compare the following advantages and disadvantages to see if flip charts are right for you:

Advantages

- Perfect for small group presentations.
- Encourage audience participation.
- Promote visual reinforcement of key points.
- Adapt to any venue.
- Easy, inexpensive way to make colorful visual aids.

Disadvantages

- Bad handwriting can spoil the prop.
- Must be replaced over time.
- Can be difficult to see.
- Can be difficult to move.

Public Speaking

In this industry, chances are, most of your presentations are made on the fly—in the elevator, on the phone, at a crowded conference hall—or to two or three middle-level executives in an empty conference, board, or interview room. But as we learned in the *Selling* section, it behooves you to start branching out into the heady world of trade organizations and the seminar circuit to garner more sales—and spread your company's message. For that reason, the following helpful tips will guide you down the challenging path of public speaking.

20 Tips for Successful Public Speaking

Feeling *some* degree of nervousness before a presentation is natural *and* healthy. However, too much nervousness can ruin all of your hard work and effort. Here are twenty quick ways in which you can start to control your nervousness and begin making effective, memorable presentations that you'll actually *enjoy*:

- **Know your material.** Practice your speech and revise it accordingly.

- **Know the venue.** Take additional steps to become familiar with the setting in which you will be presenting.

- **Know the audience.** Greet some of the audience as they arrive. It's easier to speak to a group of friends than to a group of strangers.

- **Remind.** Installing several places to recap, or remind, your audience about what you've just gone over is a great way to reorient yourself, as well as them.

- **Visualize yourself giving your speech.** Imagine yourself speaking, your voice loud, clear, and assured. When you visualize yourself as successful, you will *be* successful.

- **Realize that people *want* you to succeed.** Audiences want you to be interesting, stimulating, informative, and entertaining. They don't want you to fail.

- **Never apologize.** Don't assume that the audience picked up on something you may have left out or glossed over. Mention it, and they surely will. Keep quite about it and just move on, and they probably won't.

- **Don't rely on "tricks."** Your focus should be on the message, not the venue, the visuals, the microphone, or the auditorium's sound system.

- **Turn nervous energy into positive energy.** Harness your nervous energy and transform it into vitality and enthusiasm for your subject.

- **Gain experience.** Experience builds confidence, which is the key to effective speaking. A Toastmasters club can provide the experience you need.

- **Make eye contact**. Use eye contact with each member of the audience in turn.

- **Empathize with the audience**. Your audience is often as nervous as you are. By putting them at ease, you will have the same effect on yourself.

- **Keep visual aids simple**. Remember, less is more. Visual aids are a tool, not a crutch. Have just enough to convey, not confuse.

- **Have an agenda**. Not just a mental one, but a printed one as well. This keeps both you and the audience on schedule, and on task.

- **Trust the audience**. Remember: You are not alone. Realize that the audience is not "out to get you," and that they have a responsibility as well. Their professionalism and attentiveness will help you to succeed.

- **Visualize your success**. Don't think, "How can I survive this?" Think, "How can I do this brilliantly?"

- **Don't dwell on the negative**. Rather than thinking, "I hope I don't screw up," take steps to *excel*.

- **Vary your voice**. Rehearse your speech as if you were an actor. Find appropriate places to pause, speak quietly, speak loudly, etc. Your audience will stay on its toes, and be more likely to stay attentive.

- **Relax**. Learn how to control your nerves through exercise, meditation, or several of the options we've included throughout this chapter.

- **Read**. Many speakers rely solely on themselves to solve the critical problem of presenting. But why ignore help when it's already out there? In addition to this one, there already exist many good books on the subject of public speaking. Read one, and *learn*.

10 Fears of a Public Speaker

So what exactly *are* people afraid of when it comes to public speaking? Here's a list of the top ten:

- Being heckled.
- Veering so far off track you don't know how to get back on.
- Going blank altogether.
- Having a loud, obnoxious, "know-it-all" in the audience.
- Not being able to hide obvious signs of nervousness (sweat, trembling, etc.).
- Having an audience talk over you.
- Messing up—horribly—while being videotaped.
- The impossible to answer "Question from Hell."
- Having an audience walk out on you.
- You running out on the audience . . .

Taking the Fear out of Public Speaking

Finally, it should be noted that public speaking ranks at the very top of most people's "10 Most Hated Things to Do" list. And as we saw in the list on the previous pages, there's plenty of reason to be afraid. But utilizing the tools in this book will help you be more prepared, more confident, more experienced, and more professional in your approach to public speaking.

In turn, each successful presentation will help rid your fear of this challenging and daunting task. The fact is, few "people" industries, especially commercial real estate, can avoid the role of public speaking. And if you're going to have to do it, you might as well learn how to not be afraid while doing it. Like a backyard swimming pool that's still a little chilly on the first day of summer, it's better to jump in than wade in.

So, what are you waiting for?

3 Ways to Fight a Fear of Public Speaking

There's no sin in being afraid, as long as you're constantly working on *conquering* that crippling fear. To overcome the fear of public speaking is a daunting challenge, to be sure, but here are a few ways to help:

- **Finding the Right Balance:** Find the right balance for yourself. Perhaps this means jogging, or swimming, or napping, or meditation. Or a combination of all four, or only two. The trick is to keep trying new things until you find those that fit. In the *trying*, perhaps you'll notice that one component is finally missing: your *fear*!

- **Distract Yourself:** Play a long round of golf, then have dinner with friends, then read a sizzling bestseller before going to bed. Finding ways to distract yourself could just be the ticket to conquering your fear once and for all.

- **Staying Positive:** Staying positive is not something we "should" do, it's something we must do. But it's not an automatic response, like breathing. It's something we must learn to do, or perhaps the more appropriate term is to *re*-learn to do. After all, as children, few of us felt anything *but* positive.

Sample Speech Outline

Giving a formal presentation to a large audience numbering between 30-300 people requires different planning than your usual "elevator conference" or informal gathering of two to three decision-makers. Though the word "speech" has gotten a bad rap over the years, the following speech outline will help you better prepare for the formality and length of a mass presentation:

A. Opening

  1. Captures the audience's attention

  2. Leads into the speech topic

B. Body

  1. First point
      a. Statement of fact
      b. Supporting material

  2. Second point
      a. Statement of fact
      b. Supporting material

  3. Third point
      a. Statement of fact
      b. Supporting material

  4. Repeat points until your message is clear . . .

C. Conclusion

  1. Review or summary

  2. Call to action or memorable statement

Michael J. Lipsey

Dealing with Difficult Audience Members

Branching out from smaller, informal presentations to speaking in public, such as to a trade show or seminar audience, brings with it a whole new set of benefits. Similarly, there are also brand new downfalls to contend with. One of the biggest negatives to public speaking is the "difficult" audience member.

But rest assured, if you are being annoyed by a disruptive guest, so will the rest of your audience. In general, audiences are very polite and professional in such situations, and with a few of the following simple steps, you will have the situation back under control in no time:

- Request at the beginning of your speech that guests raise their hand before making any comments or questions.

- If someone does begin interrupting your presentation, firmly remind them of your opening remarks. Most people will respond instantly to this.

- If this interruption persists, quickly revise your opening remarks to say that you will respond to all questions "at the end of my presentation."

- If someone totally disputes your point of view, avoid a one-to-one debate. Rather, set a time limit of three to five minutes and open up the floor for general debate.

The Five "Be's" of Handling Tough Questions

Another downside to speaking to large audiences is the greater risk of "tough questions." But tough questions, like tough audience members, can be converted from an asset to a liability if you follow just a few of the following steps. These are the Five "Be's" of Handing Tough Questions:

- **Be Honest**: Admit to a tough questioner that you honestly don't know something and promise to find out for them.

- **Be Busy**: Remind him or her that you have limited time and a lot to cover.

- **Be Polite**: Ask a persistent questioner—politely—to see you later for further discussion.

- **Be Firm**: You don't have to answer questions immediately or on the questioner's terms. Answer questions after your presentation or during a break.

- **Be ... the Boss**: Always remember that YOU are the speaker and THEY are the audience. While they may also be potential customers, no prospect wants to deal with a presenter who doesn't have control. The best way to have control, is to "be the boss."

7 Ways to Use Humor in Your Presentation

Nothing sets an audience—or a speaker—at ease like the use of appropriate humor in an otherwise serious presentation. But like other facets of presenting, there's a fine line between using humor—and abusing it. To avoid making this critical mistake, here are some simple guidelines to follow:

- **Avoid sensitive topics**. Religion, race, political scandal, past, present, and future presidents, prayer in schools, etc., may get a laugh, but might just turn some audience members off. Don't risk it.

- **Avoid jokes that cater to a particular sex**. Today's business world is co-ed. Don't alienate one sex by making fun of another.

- **Be yourself**. If you're not comfortable telling *jokes*, tell stories or personal anecdotes instead.

- **Find good jokes**. Funny jokes, poems, and toasts are all the rage in bookstores and card shops these days. Why not borrow material that you already *know* will work?

- *Deliver* **your jokes**. A joke does not tell itself. You must deliver a joke.

- **Test your jokes first**. Try your jokes out on colleagues, spouses, and friends. If they don't laugh, chances are nobody else will either.

- **Remove jokes that don't work**. Finally, if a joke just doesn't work, on several audiences, get rid of it. Period.

PART THREE:

COMMERCIAL REAL ESTATE NEGOTIATION

Michael J. Lipsey

Introduction

Many practitioners see the entire negotiating process as a roadblock, an obstacle. Top Performers recognize this delicate tightrope act as a golden **opportunity**. They know that during this intimate process—perhaps more than at any other time during a sale—there is ample opportunity to learn more about, and get to know, a prospect.

"Prepare by knowing your walkway (conditions) and by building the number of variables you can work with during the negotiation. You need to have a walkway ... a combination of price, terms, and deliverables that represents the *least* you will accept. Without one, you have no negotiating road map . . ."

—Keiser

The Negotiating chapter of *Systems for Success* was developed to specifically address the day-to-day issues that face the modern broker during real estate negotiations. Like the previous chapters, **Selling** and **Presenting**, negotiating is a learned skill that is well within the reach of anyone—and this chapter provides "take-aways" that can be implemented immediately. The tips, ideas, and strategies presented will radically improve your ability to better represent the tenant through negotiated settlements by understanding the following:

- Foundations of Effective Negotiating
- The Aims of Negotiation
- Capturing the Essentials
- Resolving Problems
- Concluding with Conviction
- Negotiation Tools

Michael J. Lipsey

Due to the fact that more and more negotiations may end in deadlock under current market conditions, we will examine ways around a deadlock with strategies that work; adversarial negotiating and finding common ground; focusing on the benefits of thorough preparation; identifying needs; and surprises, costs, and questions to ask while negotiating.

Preparing To Negotiate

Much like in preparing to make a winning presentation, preparation is the key to a successful negotiation. But here the preparation runs more along the lines of gathering information about the individual or team that will be sitting across from you in the more intimate settings of modern negotiations.

In this crucial chapter you will discover:

- **The Aims of Negotiating**
- **Goals and Expectations**
- **Gathering Information**
- **Needs Analysis**
- **Assessing the Other Side (H.U.RR..I.C.A.I.N.E.)**

The many ideas and strategies that follow are designed specifically to aid you in the Negotiating Process.

Michael J. Lipsey

The Aims of Real Estate Negotiation

The primary aim of any negotiation is to produce a **lasting agreement** between **two satisfied parties**. The broker can only achieve this delicate balance when trained in the negotiation process. Here you will learn all the skills required to master this intricate art, beginning with the aim of the negotiation process itself.

2 Signs of a Lasting Agreement

As we have seen, the main goal of negotiating is a lasting agreement between two satisfied parties. The agreement lasts only when two qualifiers are met:

- **Both Sides Honor It:** A broken agreement is no better than "no" agreement. Making sure that both sides honor an agreement should be at the heart of every step of the negotiating process.

- **There is No Unpleasant "Aftermath":** Bound by the agreement, both sides should reap various benefits and be completely satisfied with the results. To that end, crafting a mutually exclusive agreement should play a major role in any negotiation.

3 Types of Agreement Satisfaction

A mutually beneficial agreement lasts only because all sides are satisfied with it. Three kinds of satisfaction are necessary to sustain a lasting agreement, and secure future dealings with a satisfied tenant:

- **Process**: Regardless of the outcome, all parties feel the negotiation process was fair and orderly—and they would use the process again.

- **Substance**: All parties feel that their primary interests have been met to the maximum degree possible—given other parties' needs—and have accepted substitutes where necessary.

- **Emotional**: All parties feel better with the outcome than they felt *before* the conflict was resolved.

5 Steps to Preparing for Any Negotiation

Preparing for a successful negotiation involves more than just research. To get to know the individual or team you are negotiating with, it helps to know yourself. And vice versa. Here are five ways to prepare for a successful negotiation:

- **Take stock of your weaknesses.** Not everyone is born with the inherent skills of a great negotiator. Admitting that you're not an expert is a wonderful motivator for learning more—and *becoming* one!

- **Determine your bottom-line goal.** Before you can negotiate effectively, you must identify the **one** thing you must come away with. Don't have a shopping list of possible objectives, zero in on one and focus on that. This will guide the negotiating process instead of bogging it down.

- **Learn as much as possible about the other party.** If you're negotiating with a business, collect company brochures, annual reports, trade journals, and newspapers that cover local business news. In addition, you can search the Internet and commercial databases for information on who else might be negotiating for the same thing you're after.

- **Establish a relationship** *before* **the negotiation begins.** The worst place to meet an individual is at the negotiation table. If at all possible, try to get to know them on a personal level. Arrange a casual lunch or dinner, pick the other party up at the airport, or simply chat over the phone.

- **Create—and stick to—an agenda.** No matter how experienced a broker is, negotiations often assume a life of their own, veering off into areas unrelated to your core objective. Formulating an agenda helps keep the discussion on track.

6 Barriers to a Successful Negotiation

Another important aspect of preparing for a successful negotiation is playing devil's advocate. This involves realizing—and preparing for—the potential barriers to negotiation. Here are six such barriers to consider:

- **Confronting Instead of Negotiating:** Negotiation need not be confrontational. If you are confrontational, you will have a fight on your hands. Instead, remember that the most effective form of negotiation is characterized by both parties working *together* to find a mutually satisfying solution.

- **"Winning" Instead of** *Succeeding***:** Try not to view negotiation as a contest that must be won. When there is a winner, there must also be a "loser." The best perspective in negotiation is to try to find a solution where **both** parties "win."

- **Letting Emotions Get the Best of You:** It's normal to become emotional during a negotiation. However, it is important to maintain control. As we get more emotional, we are less able to channel our negotiating behavior in constructive ways.

- **Not Having Empathy:** If we don't know what the person needs or wants, we will be unable to negotiate properly. Often, when we take the time to find out about the other person, we discover an alternative solution that might not have otherwise existed.

- **Getting Personal:** When faced with a difficult or obnoxious person, we have a tendency to get off track by focusing on their negative personality traits. Once this happens, effective negotiation is all but impossible. Stick to the issues, and put aside your personal feelings of dislike for the individual.

- **Placing Blame:** Blame implies guilt, and guilt implies a guilty *party*. Instead of placing blame, take responsibility. In this way, you will create a spirit of cooperation.

8 Ways to "BE" a More Effective Negotiator

The ability to negotiate successfully is crucial for survival in today's changing business world. Negotiating is a complex process, but one worth mastering. If you keep in mind that you are responsible for the success or failure of negotiation, and if you follow the eight tips below, you will find it that much easier to **BE**-come a better negotiator:

- **BE Prepared**. In order to negotiate effectively, efficiently, and wisely, it is crucial to **prepare**. Doing your homework can save a lot of time. Preparation means understanding the short- and the long-term consequences you use and the results you pursue.

- **BE Conscious . . .** of the difference between positions and interests. Interests are the building blocks of lasting agreements. If you can figure out why you want something—and why others want their outcome—then you are looking at interests, and not positions.

- **BE Creative**. Anyone can do things the same old way. If you respond with new ideas and do the unexpected, you can open doors to far greater gains than when you behave predictably. A little creativity can make *everyone* look good.

- **BE Fair**. If people feel a process is fair, they are more likely to make real commitments and less likely to walk away with an unsatisfactory—and unrealistic—agreement.

- **BE Prepared to Commit**. You shouldn't make a commitment unless you can fulfill it. In fact, a mutual commitment is not likely to result unless all parties feel the process has been fair.

- **BE an Active Listener**. Active listening can change the rules of the game and raise the level of civility in the negotiation. Focus on what others say, both on their words and their underlying meaning. This will help you understand the interests upon which an agreement can be based.

- **BE Conscious of . . .** the importance of the relationship. Most of your negotiation is with repeaters (people you run across again and again). If you understand the relative priority of the relationship, it can be easier to know when giving in on a particular point may yield short-term costs but long-term gains.

- **BE Aware of Your "BATNA."** BATNA stands for the **B**est **A**lternative **T**o a **N**egotiated **A**greement. Your BATNA is a measure of the relative value of negotiating a particular issue with a particular party—or whether you can fall back on better alternatives.

30 Tips for Successful Real Estate Negotiating

Negotiating is an art practiced by virtually everyone; it is a craft mastered by few. There are many techniques to making negotiation work. If you pay careful attention to the following thirty factors, you should find that negotiating, with all the stakeholders who are clamoring for your attention, will yield more efficiency, less stress, and greater long-term success:

- *Everything* **is negotiable.** "Challenge" means not taking things at face value. You cannot negotiate unless you are willing to challenge the validity of the opposing position. Being assertive means asking for what you want and refusing to take "no" for an answer. Being assertive is part of negotiation consciousness.

- **Become a good listener.** Negotiators are detectives. They ask probing questions and then shut up. The other negotiator will tell you everything you need to know—all you have to do is listen. Many conflicts can be resolved easily if we learn how to listen. You can become an effective listener by allowing the other person to do most of the talking.

- **Be prepared:** Gather as much pertinent information prior to the negotiation. What are their needs? What pressures do they feel? What options do they have? Doing your homework is vital to successful negotiation.

- **Aim high:** Successful negotiators are optimists. A proven strategy for achieving higher results is opening with an extreme position. Sellers should ask for more than they expect to receive, and buyers should offer less than they are prepared to pay.

- **Be patient:** Whoever is more flexible about time has the advantage. Your patience can be devastating to the other negotiator if they are in a hurry.

- **State Your Needs:** The other person needs to know what *you* need. It is important to state not only what you need, but also why you need it. Disagreement may exist regarding the method for solving an issue, but not about the overall goal.

- **Prepare Options Beforehand:** Before entering into a negotiating session, prepare some options that you can suggest if your preferred solution is not acceptable. Anticipate why the other person may resist your suggestion, and be prepared to counter with an alternative.

- **Don't Argue:** Arguing is about trying to prove the other person wrong. Negotiating is about finding solutions. Don't waste time arguing. If you disagree with something, state your disagreement in a gentle but assertive way. Don't demean the other person or get into a power struggle.

- **Consider Timing:** There are good times to negotiate and bad times. Bad times include those situations where there is a high degree of anger on either side, preoccupation with something else, or perhaps even tiredness on one side or the other. Plan negotiations to avoid these times.

- **Focus on satisfaction.** Help the other negotiator feel satisfied. Satisfaction means that their basic interests have been fulfilled. Don't confuse basic interests with positions: Their position is what they *say* they want; their basic interest is what they really *need* to get.

- **NEVER make the first move.** The best way to find out if the other negotiator's aspirations are low is to induce them to open first. They may ask for less than you think. If you open first, you may give away more than is necessary.

- **NEVER accept the first offer.** If you do, the other negotiator will think they could have done better. (It was too easy.) They will be more satisfied if you reject the first offer—because when you eventually say "yes," they will conclude that they have pushed you to your limit.

- **Don't make unilateral concessions.** Whenever you give something away, get something in return. Always tie a string: "I'll do this—*if* you do that." Otherwise, you are inviting the other negotiator to ask you for more.

- **Always be willing to walk away!** Never negotiate without options. If you depend too much on the positive outcome of a negotiation, you lose your ability to say "no."

- **Do your homework.** This goes beyond intercultural negotiations to any encounter—every negotiation requires preparation.

- **Don't rush to judgment**: Negotiations that focus on the interests and needs of both parties are more appealing than sitting in judgment or having judgment laid on you when you're negotiating.

- **No pigeonholing**: Don't pin a too-specific description on the other party, whether it is their gender, ethnicity, education, occupation, or business center—this is known as pigeonholing. The danger here is making a broad and potentially wrong assumption about someone.

- **Be flexible**: Being flexible involves knowing when certain assumptions are wrong—and letting go of them.

- **Bring it with you.** Come prepared with all necessary documents and agreements. This applies to various facts and figures, as well.

- **Arrive promptly.** Never, ever be late to a negotiation if you can avoid it. It immediately puts the opposition on the defensive, and has loads of negative connotations associated with it.

- **Be "appropriately" polite.** Maintain the formality and/or informality set by the meeting chairperson. If the CEO is informal, don't insult her by being overly formal; and vice versa.

- **Don't confuse formality with respect.** Don't let negotiating on a "casual Friday" make you lose your manners. Greet and treat *everyone* with respect, always. Always.

- **Be likeable.** If the opposing side likes you, you stand a much better chance of achieving your goals within reason. However, don't make that your primary goal.

- **Keep an open mind.** It is said that an open mind is like a parachute; it must be *open* to be effective. Listen actively and keep an open mind rather than deal from a position of entrenched antagonism.

- **Keep your emotions in check.** The other side will try to make you lose your cool to gain the controlling edge. Don't let them.

- **Don't browbeat, denigrate, or insult the opposing team.** Remember the Golden Rule: "Do unto others as you would have them do unto you."

- **Deflect rather than respond to personal attacks.** The best way to achieve this is to remain calm. "Killing them with kindness," is sometimes the best approach to take with an angry or abusive prospect.

- **Resist placing blame.** Don't insist that the opinions and positions of the opposing team are "wrong." Suggest that they look at it from another perspective.

- **Don't threaten.** Most threats are empty, few can be backed up, and none are EVER an effective bargaining tool.

- **Cooperate rather than agitate.** The best way to approach any negotiation is as a team effort. Not your team versus theirs, but all of you in the struggle together.

6 "Intangibles" That Affect Negotiation

For all the planning you put into your upcoming negotiation, there are always "intangibles," things you can't see or feel that affect the outcome. Intangibles are often the key factors in many negotiations. Some of these intangibles include:

- **Lack of enthusiasm:** A lack of facial expressions, vocal intonation, and other cues can result in a negotiation breakdown. Constantly reiterate your interest in the other side's concerns and your determination to find a mutually satisfactory resolution.

- **Personality conflicts:** Be conscious of aspects of your personality such as your own needs and interpersonal style as well as the other person's personality. These factors will play a key role and understanding yourself will be an important factor.

- **Your own unique style**: Remember that during any negotiation, you have an audience. This is not the time to be "free and easy" with your own personal style. Gauge your energy level, movements, and enthusiasm by the person across the table from you and adjust yourself accordingly.

- **Physical space:** Where are you meeting? Is the temperature comfortable for both you and your guest? Have you done all you can to make the room as non-threatening as possible?

- **Past interaction:** If there is a history of conflict resolution with this person, think about how this history might affect the upcoming negotiation

- **Time pressure:** Think about whether time pressure will affect the negotiation and whether you need to try to change this variable?

Goals & Expectations of the Real Estate Negotiation

You cannot know when to say "yes" and when to say "no" without first knowing what you are trying to achieve. And research on setting goals discloses one simple but powerful fact:

> **The more specific your vision of what you want and the more committed you are to that vision, the more likely you are to obtain it.**

To become an effective negotiator, you must find out where you want to go—and why. It also means taking the time to transform your goals from simple targets into genuine expectations.

5 Priorities to Remember When Setting Goals

Like everything else in the negotiation process, setting goals is not enough. You must learn to set realistic, achievable goals that are mutually beneficial for you and your prospect. Here are five priorities to remember when setting goals:

- **Prioritize.** Think about what you and your tenant really *want* out of the agreement.

- **Set an optimistic—but justifiable—target.** Just be sure you can back it up with facts and figures.

- **Be specific.** Grandiose themes and high ideals don't belong at the bargaining table. Leave them behind and bring one unifying goal to the table instead.

- **Get committed.** Write down your goal and, if possible, discuss the goal with your tenant.

- **Deliver.** Carry your goal with you into the negotiation.

4 Goals for a First Meeting

First meetings are a golden opportunity to mine the prospect for information, motivation, and inspiration. The broker must determine how to satisfy the primary interests of the tenant to the maximum degree possible given the other party's needs in order to manage a sustainable outcome. This is achieved through rigorous preparation, planning, and needs analysis to meet the tenant's needs and objectives.

It is wise to avoid presenting or responding to positions when meeting with the other parties for the first time. Treat the first meeting as you would the "warm-up" stage of the selling process. Instead of "winning," concentrate more on the following four goals of a first meeting:

1. Defining Issues

- Ask the right questions
- Ask open-ended questions

2. Defining Interests

- Know their industry to ask the right questions
- Explore their issues and what their problems may be

3. Establishing Trust

- Share expectations fully and openly
- Identify areas of potential conflict
- Plan ways to achieve the shared goals

4. Establish Rapport

- Listening
- Disclosing
- Pacing

5 Ways to Research a Prospect

It is a key step when negotiating with a new prospect to know as much as possible about the potential tenant beforehand. This is done through careful research using a variety of sources. Consider doing the following the next time you negotiate with someone for the very first time:

- Interview the organization executives in charge of the event
- Interview a sampling of the negotiating team
- Review company literature
- Research industry news via the Internet, magazines, newspapers, etc.
- Research associates within the industry

Getting to "KNOW" in 5 Quick Steps

The most effective form of research is that which is the most targeted for a beneficial outcome. The following are five things every negotiator should KNOW before his or her next meeting with a prospect:

- **KNOW Your Target.** What equals a "bulls eye" for you? How about them? Narrowing in on an equally beneficial outcome is crucial for the planning for—and success of—any negotiation.

- **KNOW About Timing.** Pick your time carefully. When you asked Dad for a loan, did you hit him up right when he walked in the door or did you wait until after he'd had his dinner and was in a good mood? Like anything else, a major aspect of negotiation is good timing.

- **KNOW the Company.** What percentage did profits, sales, and market share increase last year? Decrease? Be voracious in your research of a new prospect, or even an existing one with new developments, to be better prepared for your negotiation.

- **KNOW the Competition.** What are other people at other companies charging for the same service? More than you? Less? What services do they provide? How do you do it better? Worse? How can you improve? How can they? These are all vital questions to answer for yourself—and your prospect—before a negotiation begins.

- **KNOW Your Product(s).** Stay on top of EVERYTHING that happens in your company and take nothing for granted. Find a key person in every department and check in regularly to get the latest updates—then pass them along to your prospect.

Needs Analysis

As is so important when selling, it is equally essential in negotiating to have as much information as possible about the other side's needs, abilities, and expectations. Much of this information will not be available except directly "from the horse's mouth." Your opportunity for a successful negotiation lies in the **un-articulated** and **un-served** sections of the following illustration.

C
L Unarticulated   *Unexploited* O
I   p
E   p
N   o
T   Articulated Today's   r
                        Business t
N   u
E   n
E   i
D   Served   Unserved t
S   i
                                  e
                                  s

CLIENT TYPES

6 Pre-Meeting Goals

In advance of the first meeting in any ongoing negotiation process, it is important to identify the concepts, terms, conditions, reasons, and other elements you want to clarify. These key components will help you prepare questions to insert at specific points in the discussion. Also anticipate that the other side will probe *you* for the same kind of information. Here are six critical questions you should ask, and expect to be asked:

- What do you want to learn from the other side?
- How will you find it out?
- What kind of questions (opened, closed, leading, etc.)?
- What specific questions do you anticipate from the other side?
- What will you let them know?
- What do you want them to know, and how will you reveal it?

H. U. R. R. I. C. A. I. N. E.

The tools you have been provided with so far are all useful in learning to identify your negotiating position. Prior to entering the actual negotiating phase itself, determining your position will assist you in your preparation. Using the **HURRICAINE Rating System**, you can determine which side of the negotiating table is stronger in the power factors and focus on increasing your strength prior to entering this phase.

Consider which side is stronger in the power factors and assign a number to each team for each item. The total points for any item is 5, i.e., for "Understanding," if you give one side 4 you must give the other side 1.

After rating all items, total the points for both teams at the bottom and compare. The totals will range between 0 and 50. The team with the higher **HURRICAINE** rating is more likely to have its way in the negotiation, unless the other team works much harder or is able to achieve a tactical upset of the power balance. Note that two of the items (*Investment* and *Need*) are negative in impact, since they decrease flexibility.

- **HARM:** The side that can cause greater damage to the other's image, economic situation, or functionally is stronger.

- **UNDERSTANDING:** The side that understands the deal points, has better information, and is using logic is stronger.

- **RESOURCES:** The larger party with more time, money, and people to devote to the negotiation is stronger.

- **REWARD:** The side with more to offer in terms of direct benefits, future business, publicity, or referrals is stronger.

- **INVESTMENT**: The side that has invested more effort, time, money, image, or ego has more to lose and is therefore weaker.

- **CREATIVITY:** The side that can create more acceptable options during the negotiation is stronger.

- **ABILITY:** The side with smarter, more experienced, more knowledgeable, and more skillful people is stronger.

- **INFLUENCE:** The side who can use more external forces such as publicity, centers for influence, public or professional groups, or high-level leaders is stronger.

- **NEED:** The side that can least afford an impasse, the side that wants and needs to make the deal, is weaker.

- **EMPHASIS:** The side who has assigned a higher internal priority, who has more focus, and internal unity and a clearer strategy, is stronger.

Michael J. Lipsey

The Negotiating Process

Negotiating is the process by which two or more parties with different needs and goals work to find a mutually acceptable solution to an issue. Because negotiating is an inter-personal process, each negotiating situation is different, and influenced by each party's skills, attitudes, and style.

We often look at negotiating as unpleasant because it implies conflict. However, negotiating need not be characterized by bad feelings or angry behavior. Understanding more about the negotiation process allows you to manage your negotiations with confidence—and increases the chance that the outcome will be positive for both parties involved. The following skills are designed to do just that . . .

7 Fundamental Truths of Negotiation

Most negotiating pros would agree that before entering a negotiation, it's important to recognize a few underlying principles:

- **Avoiding Excess Baggage.** People, not companies, sit down at the bargaining table, and each negotiator comes with a set of viewpoints and emotions—otherwise known as "baggage." If you dislike an opponent's personal baggage, be careful not to transfer that negative attitude onto the substantive issues of the negotiation.

- **Back-Story.** Most negotiators do their homework on the *issues*, but fall short when it comes to figuring out the *opponent*. Use our **HURRICAINE** tool to assess the strengths and weaknesses of the other side, then place a few phone calls to people who have dealt with your adversary to discover other idiosyncrasies of an opponent. This "back story" will be all the more helpful when the two of you finally sit down together.

- **Walking Point.** Your demeanor should suggest that you want a deal, but you don't *need* a deal. Always be prepared to walk away if you can't get what you want. When people know you're prepared to walk away, they are much more likely to make concessions to see that you don't.

- **Bargaining Chips.** The give-and-take of negotiation should result in a mutually beneficial agreement. When opponents feel victimized, they many not uphold an agreement or may be impossible to deal with in the future. Good negotiators realize that money isn't the only issue in negotiations and have a fistful of items to ask for—and to give away. These bargaining chips are designed to "sweeten the deal," without blowing it.

- **Question & Answer.** Open-ended questions allow you to look behind your opponents' position and uncover their underlying thinking. For example, if someone says that your price is too high, you respond with, "**Why** do you say that?" These are the types of open-ended questions you should be willing to ask to move the negotiation along. (Refer to the chapter on *Selling* for more information on "Questioning Techniques.")

- **Vocabulary.** As in any business dealings, your language should be respectful but not offensive. Making "suggestions" and "recommendations" is far better than making "demands" or saying, "take it or leave it."

- **Power Plays.** One side usually doesn't hold all the cards, and power in negotiation exists to the extent that it is perceived and accepted. If the deck is definitely stacked against you, you can create your own power by concentrating on your strengths and by showing that you have lots of options, since more options equal more power.

10 Tactics of Negotiating

Part of preparing for any negotiation is structuring your *aims* of negotiating. What goals do you have? What difficulties do you foresee? What is the end game? What do you visualize leaving the table with?

As we have shown in previous chapters, thorough *preparation* and *practice* are the real keys to success. Below are some of the most powerful pointers we've discovered for focusing your aims during any negotiation:

- *Know* **your walk-away alternatives.** Make sure that you have real, viable options in case the prospect doesn't extend an acceptable agreement. Your confident attitude will compel others to listen to—and eventually meet—your interests.

- **Do not** *disclose* **your walk-away alternatives.** When you give an ultimatum, your commitment to negotiation falls into question, and the environment quickly turns hostile. This draws the attention away from underlying needs, and the climate becomes less conducive to the development of creative options.

- **Figure out the walk-away alternatives of the** *other* **party.** Knowing what options the other side has if no agreement is reached will help you construct options that are favorable to both parties.

- **Analyze the offer before reacting.** Any offer is valid as long as it is mutually beneficial to both sides. Too high or too low are relative to the services you will adjust accordingly.

- **Don't sink to their level.** When you encounter tactics intended to intimidate, rush, draw out discussions, or otherwise derail the focus from underlying needs and mutual gain, patiently react to the problem at hand.

- **Prioritize.** Focus time on building an understanding of which needs are most likely to influence the outcome. Strive to create options that satisfy those interests.

- **Listen more, talk less.** As a listener, you are gathering information that can help you figure out which of the other side's needs must be met for an agreement to be considered acceptable, and to what degree those needs will have to be met. Listening gives you the advantage.

- **Know "who's who" in the room**. Make sure you know whether or not you are negotiating with a gatekeeper—or a decision-maker.

- **Analyze concessions.** Look for patterns in the types of concessions made by the other parties, and be attentive to the messages sent by your concessions. When the other side makes a concession on the terms of a specific issue, it is statistically certain that a second concession on the same issue can be secured.

- **Avoid feeling guilt.** When an apparent impasse has been reached, "splitting the difference" is widely regarded as the ultimate fair solution. But the suggestion to split the difference is often used to induce guilt. Guilt is likely to lead to concessions on *your* part— not theirs.

10 Negotiating Tactics (And Their Neutralizers)

Recognizing—and neutralizing—a defensive negotiating tactic during negotiations will allow you to get to the main objective: making a deal! But this task is one of the most difficult in the entire arena of negotiating. Here are ten negotiating tactics—and their neutralizers:

Tactic: Big Pot/Overload

    They ask for more than they expect to receive.

Neutralizer: Find out what they *really* want.

Tactic: The Bogey

    "I love you, but…" Trade emotion for economics.

Neutralizer: The Mirror – "I love you too, but…"

Tactic: The Bone

    Give concessions now…we have more big business down the road.

Neutralizer: Contract for the future business or give credit.

Tactic: Car Salesman/Plateau Negotiating

    They create the perception that you got a great deal!

Neutralizer: See the "wizard" for yourself.

Tactic: Cherry-Picking

    Obtain bids from several area competitors – pick best of all to make you compete against them.

Neutralizer: Ask for specifics and/or Present Your Features and Benefits

---

Tactic: The Crunch or 11th Hour Squeeze

    They don't sign the lease! They wait for you to give up more concessions.

Neutralizer: Empty Cupboard (there isn't anything left), Moral Appeal (prepare in advance for this), or Reversal (what do we get in return – high risk)

Tactic: Emotion

The angry parent surfaces!

Neutralizer: Humor (high risk), Enter Your Angry Parent (high risk), or Don't Get Hooked – stay in your adult state.

Tactic: Ice Pick

Lead you to believe you are very close to the deal "Hidden Agenda & The Good Cheerleader."

Neutralizer: Don't get sucked in early (get notes prior to meeting) or "The Salami" (what else is on their mind before you commit).

Tactic: The Nibbler

The negotiation is almost done and they ask for one concession at a time over a period.

Neutralizer: Moral Appeal or Give and Take

Tactic: The Note Taker

Intimidate by taking notes, takes your words out of context, selective listener

Neutralizer: Put your points in context.

13 Tactics to Improve Your Bargaining Performance

Every negotiator, even the very "top" of the Top Performers, has some room for improvement. Perhaps you do, too. To help you out, here are 13 Tactics to Improve Your Bargaining Performance:

- **Think "win-win," not just "win."** No one likes to lose, especially a prospect. But nor should you. Strive for deals in which both sides do better—but you do the best of all.

- **Ask more questions than you think you should.** Other people have a variety of needs; they do not always want the same things you do. If you can understand what is really important to them, they will give you more of what is important to you.

- **Rely on standards.** Reasonable people respond well to arguments based on their standards and norms. Don't be too quick to use a leverage-based approach to negotiation when a standards-based approach will work just as well.

- **Be reliable.** Keep your word. You may have a tendency to cut corners when you see victory just ahead. But other people notice if you break your promises, even over little things. And they have long memories.

- **Don't haggle when you can negotiate.** Identify the issues, fears, and risks that are most important to the other party and address their interests and priorities in exchange for accommodations on the things you want most. Package your trade-offs using the "if / then" formulation well known to negotiation experts: "If you give us what we want on issues 1 and 2, then we might consider concessions on issues 3 and 4."

- **Always acknowledge the other party.** People are proud. They like to hear you say they have some leverage, even when they don't. Don't gloat when you are the more powerful party. Treat people on the other side with appropriate respect. That does not cost much, and they will appreciate it.

- **Avoid concentrating too much on your "bottom line."** Spend extra time preparing your goals and developing high expectations. Your bottom line is exactly what you get. People who expect more *get* more. Refocus your thinking on your goals and expectations. Consider carefully what you want and why you want it.

- **Develop a specific alternative as a fallback if the negotiation fails.** There is always an alternative. Find out what it is, and bring it along with you to the bargaining table. You will feel more confident.

- **Get an agent and delegate the negotiation task.** If you are up against professional, competitive negotiators, you may be at a disadvantage. Find a more competitively oriented person to act as your agent or at least join your team. This is neither an admission of failure *or* lack of skill. It is simply prudent and wise.

- **Bargain on behalf of someone or something else, not yourself.** Even competitive people feel weaker when they are negotiating on their own behalf. Think about other people and causes—your family, your staff, even your future "retired self"—that are depending on you to act as their agent and "bring home the bacon" in this negotiation. Then bargain on *their* behalf.

- **Create an audience.** People negotiate more assertively when other people are watching them. That is why labor negotiators are so tough—they know the union rank and file are watching their every move. Tell a coworker about the negotiation, and include them on your "team."

- **Stand your ground.** Practice pushing back a little when others make a bargaining move. A simple phrase that works is "You'll have to do better than that because..." (fill in a reason). The better the reason, the better you will feel about it, *but any truthful reason will do.* Many people will respond favorably if you make a request in a reasonable tone of voice and accompany it with a "because" statement.

- **Insist on commitments, not just agreements.** Don't be so trusting. Agreements are fine if you have a solid basis for believing that the other party's word is its bond. If you don't know the people on the other side well or you suspect that they may be untrustworthy, set up the agreement so they have something to lose if they fail to perform.

10 Keys to Win-Win Bargaining

Getting to the "win" is the bottom line in any negotiation. But as we have already shown, when one person "wins," another "loses." Unless, that is, you master the fine art of "win-win" bargaining. Here are eleven ways you can start right now:

- Orient yourself toward a win-win approach
- Plan and have a concrete strategy: be clear on what is important to you and why it is important
- Know your **BATNA** (**B**est **A**lternative **T**o a **N**egotiated **A**lternative)
- Separate people from the problem
- Focus on interests, not positions; consider the other party's situation
- Create options for Mutual Gain
- Generate a variety of possibilities before deciding what to do
- Aim for an outcome based on some objective standard

- Pay a lot of attention to the flow of negotiation

- Take the Intangibles into account; communicate carefully

- Use Active Listening Skills; rephrase, ask questions—and then ask some more

11 Tactics to Increase Your Negotiating Advantage

Though few would like to admit it, negotiation is really a power struggle. Who has it? Who wants it? Who has more? Who has less? What do they do with it? Etc. To increase your negotiating advantage, here are eleven winning tactics to employ:

- **Neutral Territory**: Suggest an off-site location to equalize the position of power.

- **Enthusiasm**: Enthusiasm isn't negotiable, but it is contagious.

- **Expectation**: When you raise your expectations, you will get more.

- **Fax Machine**: During telephone negotiations, take notes and then fax them to the prospect to ensure that nothing was overlooked. Ask them to initial the notes and then fax them back.

- **News**: If video clips that support your presentation are available, get a copy to use.

- **Newspapers**: Most major newspapers have on-line archives that you can search by keyword.

- **Pay In Advance**: Arrange in advance to pay for your prospect's meal. Slip your credit card to the waiter before the meeting and request a bill not be presented.

- **Questions**: Knowing what questions to ask gives you the edge.

- **References**: Provide a list of references that are willing to validate your position.

- **Success Stories**: Share your success stories, but be careful not to brag.

- **Testimonials**: Any time a tenant compliments you or your firm, ask if they would put that comment on a sheet of their letterhead, and send it to you as a testimonial letter.

(Adapted from *Guerrilla Negotiating* by Jay Conrad Levinson, Mark S.A. Smith, and Orvel Ray Wilson)

14 Reasons People are Willing to Pay More

When it all boils down, your prospect will make a firm decision on the price of your offer. But don't lowball an offer. Many tenant s are willing to pay more than *you* think the market demands. Here are some of the reasons your prospect will be willing to pay you more than they pay your competition:

- **Company Stability**: Savvy customers will select a technically and financially sound vendor over one that is obsolete or on the brink of failure.

- **Fewer Headaches**: Your prospect will pay more to eliminate and avoid headaches.

- **Knowledgeable Sales Force**: Buyers worry when a company representative does not know the product or the industry.

- **Reputation**: When your prospect is uncertain of the market, they tend to select the vendor with the best reputation.

- **Partnership**: Savvy buyers know that the best vendor becomes a partner in their mutual success.

- **Consistency**: Consistent quality, delivery, service, and constant innovation create exceptional value in a negotiation.

- **Authority**: If you are the leader, the inventor, or the authority in the industry, you have additional power.

- **Popularity**: Many people are influenced by what is fashionable.

- **Exclusive Features**: Experienced negotiators seek exclusivity as a negotiating advantage.

- **Higher Quality**: Experienced negotiators translate higher quality to higher value.

- **Scarcity**: Anything considered scarce is considered more valuable.

- **Short Delivery Times**: When you can shorten your delivery times you gain an advantage.

- **Problems Fixed Quickly**: Rapid reaction reaps rich rewards.

- **Socially, Morally, Ethically Superior**: Many people select vendors based on these traits.

(Adapted from *Guerrilla Negotiating* by Jay Conrad Levinson, Mark S.A. Smith, and Orvel Ray Wilson)

10 Ways to Establish Trust With your Commercial Real Estate Client

Many negotiations end in deadlock because a broker didn't establish sufficient trust with his prospect. Establishing trust is essential to your success in any negotiation. Once you have developed trust and rapport, you've actually got the hard part behind you. The bottom line to negotiating is that people *want* to do business with a broker that they relate to and that they feel understands their needs. Here are some critical ways to build trust.

- **Body Language.** Be mindful of your body language and remember to keep gestures positive! Unfold your arms, uncross your legs, show your palms, and remember to *smile*.

- **Create Harmony.** "Matching and Mirroring" your prospect's body language gestures will psychologically cause them to identify with you. The power behind this principle is firmly grounded in the precept that people trust people that they believe are similar to them. This is one sure way to create harmony.

- **Act Interested.** Remember to make eye contact and listen with genuine interest. You are certain to create an unfavorable impression if you give your prospect the idea that you are not fully present in the conversation. Often, restating in your own words what the prospect has just said serves to clarify communication.

- **Control Your Impulse to INTERRUPT.** Keep your attention focused on your prospect and avoid the temptation to interrupt and dominate the conversation. The quickest way to destroy trust and rapport is to interrupt another person while they are speaking. If you do interrupt, minimize the damage by apologizing and ask them to please continue.

- **Be a PRO.** Dress and act professionally. While it may seem unfair, we are judged on our appearance. Research indicates that others form a lasting impression of us within the first five minutes. Use them wisely.

- **Past Performance:** Make sure to build on past association with a given prospect, be it by yourself or another representative of your company. Repeat how effective this performance has been in the past, and how much more effective it could be in the future.

- **Flexibility:** Keep your primary object always in focus, but don't be rigid in your dealings with the folks on the other side of the table. There's a difference between giving—and giving *in*.

- **Be Sincere:** Prospects, like grandmothers, can smell insincerity a mile away. Obviously, there are times when telling the whole truth and nothing but might give away your negotiating advantage, but there is no substitute for relating to people on a purely personal level.

- **Make a Commitment:** Learning to commit is not just a problem for twenty-something singles. When negotiating, make a firm, do-able commitment and stick to it. Nothing builds trust more than results one can depend on.

- **Find the Bottom Line:** Many people treat negotiation like warfare, and smoke and mirrors abound. Cut through the haze and surprise your prospect by getting to the bottom line.

Exploring Features & Benefits, Requirements & Solutions

There may be times when you might understand your tenant's needs better than they do, but if you cannot successfully tie the benefits of your service to those needs, you will drastically reduce the chance of obtaining a commitment.

The main objective of creating a unique and attractive sales package is to provide your tenant with *solutions* in terms of features and benefits that relate directly to their identified need(s). This can be accomplished effectively in three distinct ways:

- Present details of the features and advantages of the benefits on a **point by point** basis.

- **Tie** the benefits of your product and/or service to your tenant's needs to obtain a firm commitment.

- **Specifically** explain how the benefits of your solution can meet the tenant's needs.

Matching Features to Benefits

Every feature that you are selling must have at least one benefit to the customer or it shouldn't be used in the sale. For example:

Feature/Requirement	Benefit/Solution
Office building near the airport	People flying in for a meeting at your office can spend an entire day, without having to stay overnight.
Five anchors in mall	The anchors draw people from all over the area so you will have high traffic in front of your store.
Manufacturing plant in a rural area	There is plenty of space to expand.

Exploring Payoffs

Now that you have addressed all of the prospect's objections—and illustrated the benefits that meet that prospect's needs—you must begin to expand on the benefits by exploring the payoffs of implementing the solutions you have provided. In doing so, you will ask the tenant to list the payoffs he or she envisions resulting from this agreement. This will close the gap and heighten the tenant's interest in taking action, in the following specific ways:

- Asking tenants to list payoffs forces them to focus on their situation rather than on your product or service.

- Exploring payoffs puts the process in a problem-solving mode.

- Having tenants discuss payoffs builds their conviction about the urgency or importance of their needs.

3 Questions for Identifying Payoffs

It is not always easy to identify a potential payoff. Some questions that might help in identifying payoffs include:

- How would your organization benefit if you could eliminate these problems?

- One benefit of solving the problem would be **X**, what other benefits do you see?

- What could you do differently if this problem did not exist?

6 Steps to Creating a Sense of Urgency

Top Performers know that a successful negotiation revolves around creating a sense of urgency. The difference between merely performing, and being a Top Performer, often hinges on the sense of urgency Top Performers manage to create as they close the sale. Here are several ways to capture that all-important sense of urgency:

- **The Limited Time Offer**: Failure for the prospect to buy within a certain time frame means that you lose the opportunity to get a good deal.

- **Buy Before the Price Goes Increases**: Create a sense of urgency by acknowledging the price.

- **The Clock is Always Running**: Buy it while you still have time to enjoy it.

- **Selling One of a Kind Products**: Selling something not readily available or entirely unique creates a sense of urgency when closing the sale.

- **Selling to the Highest Bidder**: Show product/service to multiple prospects, identify time frame in which to establish a bid and sell to the highest bidder (i.e. often used in foreclosures).

- **Timing is Everything**: Every good businessperson understands the importance of timing. Use this as a strong selling point to create sense of urgency.

The "V" Model

In any successful negotiation, the natural progression is to move from exploration—to advocacy. You have already established trust in the negotiation process and further identified the customer's needs. Throughout the presentation, constantly measure the customer's responses: **HEAR** the customer.

- **H**ead
- **E**mpathize
- **A**pprehend
- **R**espond

It is now time to confirm the needs and present clear solutions as a way to finalize a lasting agreement. At this point, building these "V's" of focus into your presentation will double its effectiveness.   The "V" model for negotiating works because it:

- creates a climate of acceptance

- focuses on needs

- creates interest and anticipation

- outlines benefits or solutions

- involves the tenant in solving problems

- encourages recognition of value

- review benefits

- asks for a commitment

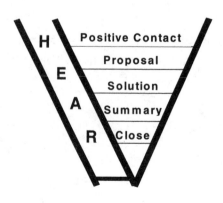

Resolving Problems that Arise During the Real Estate Negotiation

Establishing trust is not a problem; it's a *solution*. However, many times negotiation brings out the worst in people. Never forget, your main objective is to provide solutions in terms of features and benefits that relate directly to the tenant's identified need.

To accomplish that task, it is incumbent upon you to resolve problems that arise as quickly and successfully as possible. What follows are several tips and strategies on how to do just that.

8 Steps to Overcoming Objections

Every Top Performer learns to anticipate objections. You can prevent them from occurring, with preparation, practice, creativity, and focus. If you can overcome an objection before the prospect raises it, you are more likely to make a sale. Prevention is often the best way to overcome objections:

- Identify all objections
- Write them all down
- Script responses with closing questions for each
- Develop sales tools to enhance and support responses
- Rehearse in role-play with co-workers and peers
- Tweak the scripts
- Try them
- Meet as a group to discuss revisions

6 Tips for Handling Objections

Handling objections in a professional—and reasonable—manner is a skill for all negotiators to acquire, let alone Top Performers. To achieve that necessary skill, here are six useful tips for handling objections calmly, coolly, and rationally:

- **Hear them out**. Plain and simple. Nothing says, "I respect you and want to satisfy you to keep your business," like taking the time to *listen*.

- **Feed the objection back**. Great to use when several people are making the decision. Feed the objection back to the person giving the objection and let others on the team close the deal for you.

- **Question the objection**. Ask them to elaborate on their objection to find the hidden request they may be hiding.

- **Answer the objection**. Study the weaknesses of your product/service and think through ways to handle the situation. It may help to admit the shortcoming, but balance it off by comparing it to an advantage.

- **Confirm the answer**. After answering the objection, verify with your prospect that the objection has in fact been answered. Ask questions such as:

  —That clarifies this point, doesn't it?

  —This is the answer you were looking for, right?

  —With that question out of the way, we can go ahead, can't we?

- **Change gears**. Throw them a curve ball and immediately go to the next step in your selling sequence. Turn the page, step in a new direction, and introduce the next phase with a quick, "by the way."

3 Objections (and Their Hidden Requests)

Every objection is unique. In fact, very few objections "say what they mean and mean what they say." Here are a few great examples of objections with hidden requests:

- **Example 1:**

Objection: "I don't think that this represents the best value per dollar."

Hidden Request: "I challenge you to prove that your product provides an excellent value for my money."

- **Example 2:**

Objection: "I'm trying to reduce expenses, so I'm not in the market for anything new."

Hidden Request: "Unless you can convince me that your product is really something that I need, I won't buy."

- **Example 3:**

Objection: "I'm going to shop around and see what else is available."

Hidden Request: "You haven't sold me. Either keep selling so I'll be convinced to buy now, or I'm taking a walk."

10 Ways to Respond to Objections

Objections are really an opportunity for you to get in better tune with your customer's real needs. Here are ten great ways to respond to objections and still get the sale:

- Realize that objections are sales-makers, not sales-*breakers*.
- Objections show the prospect's interest.
- Understand that objections are a way to ask for additional information.
- Realize that people use minor objections to slow things down; they need time to mull things over before making a commitment.
- Determine whether hesitation is caused from an objection—or a condition.
- Keep it in perspective.

- Don't argue an objection. This could be a deal killer.
- Develop sensitivity to how prospects feel when they voice their objections.
- Show concern for "saving face."
- Lead your prospect to answer her own objection.

Objection Forecasting Matrix

Act   Confirm

The following matrix provides you with the appropriate actions to improve any objection that may be encountered while presenting.

Attitude	Likely Source	Action
Misunderstanding Indifference Changing Subject	Information	Probe, give or get correction information
Skepticism	Trust	Pace, offer proof
Impatience Delay	Style	Pace, review needs
Skepticism Denial	Substance	Substitute, refocus
Skepticism Denial Anger	Price	Review benefits

15 Ways Around A Deadlock

In the ongoing process of a successful negotiation, a deadlock is not necessarily an impasse. It may simply indicate that both sides have exhausted their creative energies and are in need of an alternative solution, perhaps from an outside party or force. Before calling off the whole deal and going back to the drawing board, consider the following fifteen alternatives around a deadlock:

- Change financial structure.
- Change team members.
- Change agenda.
- Share more risk.
- Change performance schedule.
- Offer guarantees and remedies.
- Reorganize negotiating process.
- Change legal structure.
- Call a mediator.
- Change the rules.
- Offer options.
- Change the terms.
- Adjourn and reconvene later and elsewhere.
- Reassess interests and start over.
- Involve third-party experts.

7 Ways to Deal with Difficult People During the Negotiation

Though most negotiations take place between two reasonably professional adults, it is a fact that you will occasionally wind up sitting across from a "difficult" person. When this unpleasant occasion arises, it is best to use the following tactics for dealing with them:

- **Bullies**: This is not your elementary school playground. Stand up for yourself and use self-assertive language. This gives them time to run down, thus avoiding a direct confrontation.

- **Whiners**: Listen attentively, acknowledge their feelings, and by all means avoid complaining with them. When their crying jag is over, simply state the facts without apology. They'll either provide an alternative—or take yours.

- **Stoics:** Here is where the use of questioning comes in handy. In this case, keep asking open-ended questions, but be patient in waiting for a response.

- **"Yes" Men:** In a non-threatening manner, work hard to find out why they will not take action. Be ready to compromise and negotiate, but don't allow them to make unrealistic commitments.

- **Downers:** Do not be dragged into their despair, but at the same time do not try to cajole them out of their negativism. Discuss the problem thoroughly, without offering solutions. When alternatives *are* discussed, bring up the negatives yourself. Be ready to take action alone, without their agreement.

- **Experts**. Nod in awe at their expertise and marvel at how they can "know it all." Then get down to brass tracks when they think they've sufficiently impressed you.

- **Fence Sitters.** Raise the issue of why they are hesitant. If at all possible, remove the staller from the situation. Keep the action steps in your own hands

4 Deceptive Maneuvers (And How to Handle Them)

Unfortunately, **deceptive maneuvers** are all part of the negotiating process, but hopefully parts you won't have to run up against quite too often. If you do, however, here are four of the most common deceptive maneuvers, and how to handle them in a positive way that will get the negotiation process back on track:

- **The "Add On."** An agreement has been reached and you feel good. The other side suddenly comes up with a few extra things that they "forgot" to include. The other side knows you are most vulnerable once an agreement has been reached since you don't want to lose the deal. The requests are usually minor but a lot of "add-ons" can really "add up."

   How to Deal: Either pleasantly insist that the deal stands "as is," or firmly ask for something in return for each and every "add on" item.

- **Gatekeeper vs. Decision-Maker.** Your adversary appears to have decision-making power but states, after the negotiation is completed, that the agreement must go to "a higher authority" for approval. The deal is subsequently rejected and your agreement becomes a pawn for more negotiation.

How to Deal: Ask that the true decision-maker participate in the negotiation.

- **Good Cop/Bad Cop.** This age-old tactic presents you with two opponents: one who is unreasonable and threatening and another who is pleasant and calm. After the "bad cop" rejects your offer and storms out of the room, the "good cop" steps in to placate you and resolve the issue in a peaceful manner.

  How to Deal: As with any hostile confrontation, let the "bad cop" run out of steam and negotiate with the "good cop" instead.

- **Smoke & Mirrors.** The opponent puts forth a phony issue to distract you from the main issues and to get you to make further concessions.

  How to Deal: Try to get the fake issue set aside until more important matters are figured out.

7 Ways to Put a Positive Spin on a Negative Negotiation

Despite a negotiator's expertise, it is inevitable that a situation will invariably turn bleak. It is not easy to shift a "win-lose" situation to a "win-win," but the following are seven techniques for making a down situation look "up":

- **Lighten up.** If at all possible, reduce tension through humor.

- **Listen up.** Increase the accuracy of communication by rephrasing the other's comments to make sure you *hear* them.

- **Divvy up.** Search for ways to slice the larger issue into smaller pieces.

- **Join up.** Look for greater common goals, i.e. "we are in this together."

- **"Give" up.** Focus less on *your* position and more on a clear understanding of the other's needs—then figure out ways to move toward them.

- **Move up.** Sweeten the offer; emphasize the positives.

- **Toughen up.** Get firm and have limits.

6 Tactics for Difficult Negotiations Strategies

There is no end to the possibilities of a negative negotiation strategy emanating from the other side of the table, but there *are* several tactics for dealing with them. Here are six, for starters:

- **Detach & Diagnose**: When feelings like anger, disappointment, frustration, confusion, and resentment surface, our first reaction is to respond in kind. This is never a good idea. Instead, mentally remove yourself from the situation and think about it before you respond.

- **Listen & Acknowledge**: You are best positioned to change someone's mind after you have listened to them. People tend to close down and stick to their position until they feel heard. To avoid such hurt feelings, Listen & Acknowledge.

- **Stand Up for Yourself**: Without derailing the process, let them know what *you* need. Do so firmly yet without denigrating their viewpoint, and chances are the negotiation will progress more smoothly now that there is a "bottom line."

- **Tit for Tat**: Don't freely acquiesce to the rules of the other side— without getting something in return. Rather than counter the positions or demands shot at you, change the game to one you'd rather play.

- **Negotiate the Rules**: If negotiations disintegrate to the point of breaking down, acknowledge the situation and establish some firm ground rules—together—to get back to the negotiating process with a new set of guidelines to facilitate a successful resolution.

- **Change the Players**: If all else fails, there are times when you simply need to "change the players" at the table. Remember, you can change the dynamic of the players by adding or subtracting people on either negotiating team, or by adding a third party who can oversee the process with an objective viewpoint.

Michael J. Lipsey

The 3 Pitfalls of Negotiation

To succeed at negotiating, it sometimes helps to know what NOT to do. Negotiations are full of pitfalls, from location to time, bargaining chips to psychological ploys. Here are the three most common pitfalls of negotiation, and how to avoid them the next time you're sitting at the table:

PITFALL 1: *Low-balling First*

Even the most experienced negotiators constantly fight their instinct of "low expectations." To avoid this trap of "low-balling," encourage the other side to talk first. Even if your opponents do not put forth a concrete proposal, their opening comments establish a starting point for negotiations and allow you to tweak your plan to address their wants.

PITFALL 2: *Primary Source*

Finding alternatives is the key to successful negotiating. Negotiating with only one source weakens your hand because it eliminates your ability to find alternatives. If you have only one source to negotiate with, remind yourself that the other side, by taking the time to sit across from you, is willing to consider your needs. And understand that your best offer must outshine offers from the other side's alternative options.

PITFALL 3: *Poor (or No) Follow-up*

In negotiation, the end *never* justifies the means. After all, finalizing an agreement may not mark an end to negotiations if the terms of the deal are not met down the road. Once negotiations conclude, write up all the terms and determine who will be responsible for ensuring that each stipulation is met. Then meet them . . .

4 Great Ways to Summarize

Summarizing, otherwise known as "recapping," reminds the prospect that there is an urgency to act and that your solution is appropriate. In the *Summary* stage of the negotiation process, you will:

1. **Restate the need**
2. **Restate the solution**
3. **Review the features and benefits**
4. **Confirm acceptance of the benefits**

The 3 A's of a More Effective Closing

Closing a sale is the natural and logical outcome of an effective negotiation, and culminates with the three **A**'s: **A**sk for **A**greement and **A**ction. Asking for agreement always puts some pressure on the customer to make a decision, at which point they must take some action. Once you have delivered your Close, you should reaffirm the customer's positive decision. The customer has just made a major decision; it is natural to have doubts.

Communicate that your concern goes beyond closing the deal—that this is just the beginning of your "relationship" with your new customer. Ensure the customer that you will follow up and make sure the product/service continues to meet the customer's needs and expectations. Here are three steps to follow for a more effective closing:

- **Be concise**: Make each word count. Avoid unnecessary statements that could be misinterpreted.

- **Close with conviction**: Act as if you expect the customer to accept your proposal and do not convey uncertainty. (See the list on the following page for examples.)

- **Establish eye contact**: Ask, in a friendly way, for the commitment (the action).

30 Closing Techniques

It is no secret that Top Performers are also Consummate Closers. After all, you can't call it an actual sale until you've finally closed the deal. Yet many brokers find closing the most challenging aspect of the entire sales process. Here are 30 proven techniques to help you close the deal:

- **Alternative**: Concludes the sale by offering two or more alternatives. You offer a choice between something and something instead of something and *nothing*.

- **Assumptive/Next Step**: All top sales professionals are assumptive closers. From the beginning of the presentation to the end, they confidently assume the buyer will own, even before they receive information. (Once you hear, "What's the Next Step?", switch into the Order Form Close mode.)

- **Ben Franklin/Balance Sheet**: List of Pro's and Concerns—the oldest trick in the book, for a reason—this is most effective.

- **Compromise**: Half is better than none. Reduce the initial offer to entice the prospect to buy.

- **Don't Keep It a Secret**: After all else fails, don't keep it a secret that you want the prospect's business. Ask what it would take to get their business, and even go as far as offer to get down on your hands and knees to beg for it. Never be too proud to let people know how much you would appreciate their business.

- **Erroneous Conclusion**: Intentionally make an erroneous statement, the prospect will correct you and walk right into the sale.

- **Hard to Get It**: People want those things they can't have. Focus on: "Can you qualify?" instead of, "Do you want to buy it?"

- **Hot Button**: 80/20 rule. 80% of buying decisions will be based on 20% of the product's features. Find one or two key features that represent key benefits to the person buying your products, and push his hot button over and over again.

- **I Want to Think About It**: Ask specific questions to narrow down the generality of the statement. When a specific objection can be identified, you are in a better position to overcome the apprehension. Usually the main concern is money, at which point you can begin "The Money Close."

- **I'm Still Shopping**: Sometimes an unavoidable objection. The key to this close is to give a sound reason why the prospect should not go through the agony of locating a better value, when what they want is available right now.

- **Invitational**: Invite the prospect to "try it out." If selling Real Estate, ask how do they like it? If the answer is positive, follow with, "Great, why don't you take it." If the answer is "yes," you've got a sale, if "no," ask "Why Not?" and identify their hot buttons.

- **Lost Sale**: Pretend the presentation is over and you are leaving. Ask for suggestions to improve your presentation. Listen for real reasons for not buying and for hot buttons. Once identified, you can ask to re-explain or bring comfort levels to new issues.

- **Maybe I Should Wait/Timing is Not Right**: Perfect method to overcome procrastination or uncover smoke screen objection. Answer question with a question. Find out what would be different if they delay the purchase. Unveil examples of timing not right.

- **Major/Minor Point or Secondary**: Presumes it is easier for the buyer to make many small decisions rather than one large decision; this sets the buyer up to make positive final decision.

- **The Money**: Break financial terms into components: total investment, monthly investment, or initial investment to determine what is causing hesitancy.

- **My Lawyer or Accountant**: Suggest to begin paperwork "subject to" approval with their lawyer, accountant, or advisor. This will allow you to facilitate the details of the sale.

- **Oblique Comparison**: Compare the daily price with an object that costs the same amount—something insignificant, such as "For the price of a cup of coffee each day . . ."

- **Order Form**: Effective because as you fill out the contract, you are not directly asking the prospect to buy; you are simply making the decision for him. Use this at the beginning of your presentation.

- **Paint a Fantasy Picture**: Similar to the "Assumptive Close" because you speak to the prospect as if the positive decision has already been made, only you fill the prospect with a picture of the "dream" and tap into the emotion.

- **Puppy Dog**: Similar to the "Invitational Close," where the prospect is given a product or service to try and, if not satisfied, can return it within a certain time frame.

- **Reduction of the Ridiculous; Cost Per Day**: Bridges a gap between willingness to pay and *ability* to pay. Break cost down over time and present on a monthly, weekly, daily basis: this seems less invasive.

- **Sales Manager's Close**: Using this technique, the sales manager steps in after listening to the trainee's presentation. He introduces himself to the prospect, then asks the prospect about the trainee's presentation. With a favorable response, the sales manager then gives the contract with pen to the sales trainee to close the deal.

- **Sharp Angle; or If I Could, Would You?**: Great technique when confronted with most types of objections, also good to handle the smoke-screen objections.

- **Sell-It-With Love**: Identify the emotional aspect of the sale (husband, wife, kids) and make a strong emotional appeal with that information.

- **Similar Situation**: When working with a prospect who has an objection similar to one you've recently overcome, you can share how your resolved the conflict.

- **Solve a Problem, Don't Create a Second Problem**: The salesperson's job is to solve problems. By not offering the right solution, a second problem is created because the prospect now has to figure out how to get rid of you—and the prospect's *first* problem still isn't resolved. Be forthright, let them know you came here to solve their problems—not create new ones. How can you help?

- **Summary**: Summarize the benefits to meet the tenant's needs.

- **Trial**: Test the waters to evaluate where you are with the prospect. Ask for opinions that give you insight about the prospect's thoughts on the product/service.

- **Ultimatum**: Issue your final proposal. Deliver with confidence and strength, using the attitude that this sale will not make or break your career.

- **"Yes" Momentum**: Ask questions that require the prospect to answer "yes." Use this momentum of many "Yes's" to conclude your sale with a final "Yes."

10 Great Ways to "Conclude with Conviction"

All good things must come to an end, but when you "conclude with conviction," chances are you are just *beginning*—a healthy sales relationship with the prospect, that is. Here are ten great ways to close with conviction.

- Save time for your conclusion so you don't have to rush through it.
- Let your audience know you are about to conclude with statements such as "Finally, or "In conclusion . . ."
- Don't read your conclusion. End by looking straight at your audience.
- Keep your voice confident and strong for duration of the conclusion.
- Make your conclusion brief and to the point, and then **stop**.
- Summarize clearly the key areas you covered. (Recap!)
- Recommend specific action steps during your conclusion.
- Find some convincing statistics to use as you conclude.
- Reviews using a picture of what you want people to keep in their minds.
- Reinforce the benefits of doing what you recommend.

PART FOUR:

SERVING IN COMMERCIAL REAL ESTATE:

Strategic Customer Service

Michael J. Lipsey

Introduction

In today's highly competitive market, the quality of delivered service may be the most important determinant of customer satisfaction, retention, and return. When similar competitors within an industry are roughly matched, those that stress customer service will inevitably triumph. In the commercial real estate industry, leading edge managers recognize the obvious: Satisfied customers represent a company's most precious—and profitable—resource.

Due to this expanded emphasis on customer service, competitors must continuously devise new ways to enhance delivered services. As a result, customer demands and expectations, as well as service standards, rise exponentially. Recognizing and responding to this growing demand for dependable, innovative delivered service is essential for long-term success in the commercial real estate industry.

For the same reason that it falls as our final chapter, customer service is the final *test*. You can get everything else right, in terms of product, price, and marketing, in terms of sales, presentations, and negotiations, but unless you complete the process with excellent customer service, you run the risk of losing business to your competitors.

Service, once delivered, becomes a tangible product. In this fourth and final section of the *Systems for Success* Program, you will discover:

- **What Tenants, Customers, and Clients Value**
- **The Importance of Building Management and Services**
- **The Cost of Poor Service**
- **System for Providing Quality Service**
- **Offering Value Added Services**
- **Setting Standards**
- **Keeping the Service Promise**

5 Qualities Your Clients Value

Countless research studies have shown that clients value a specific set of qualities in their brokers and property managers. Again and again, the same set of qualities appears in study after study. Based on nationwide meetings and focus groups, customer interviews, and extensive employee surveys, here are those five consistent qualities that clients value most:

- **Service Credibility.** The credibility of your service must be unquestionable. Your service is valuable for buyers and sellers, because it is an impartial assessment of what is delivered and received.

- **Good Value.** Your diverse programs, whether funded by direct service recipients or the American taxpayer, must be of good value. You must provide clients with top quality, professional service whenever and wherever they need it.

- **Accurate and Consistent Results.** Your results must be accurate and consistent, no matter who the client or whatever the circumstance.

- **Market Responsiveness.** Your programs must be responsive to market demands. You must be committed to listening to your client's needs and responding to them in a professional manner.

- **Highly Trained Employees.** Since your clients rely on you, your employees must be highly trained professionals who are responsive to their customers, motivated, and capable of identifying and helping to prevent problems.

6 Qualities YOU Can Deliver

Matching your client's expectations with your capabilities is a fine line Top Performers in the commercial real estate industry must walk every day of the week. We've seen what customers demand; now see what you can deliver:

- **Courtesy and Respect.** Client views and needs are important, and, in return, they should be able to expect professional treatment, objectivity, and confidentiality from your company.

- **Fairness.** Clients should be treated fairly, regardless of their race, color, national origin, sex, religion, age, disability, political beliefs, and marital or familial status.

- **Clarity.** Clearly explain to your tenant what you will do, how your programs work, and who to contact for further assistance. Provide the same information in written form, perhaps in a brochure or pamphlet, and remind them to store it in a visible place.

- **Accessibility.** Be available to serve your client and to talk to individuals and organizations about your programs—whenever and wherever it is humanly possible. There is nothing worse than not being able to find a contact person in a company—especially *yours*.

- **Timeliness.** Be prompt and courteous when responding to client calls. No one can be two places at the same time, but everyone can *try*!

- **Responsiveness.** Be vigilant in responding to your clients' needs on an ongoing basis.

Michael J. Lipsey

Tenant Attitudes About 9 Building Features, Amenities & Services

Recently, approximately 20,000 office tenants participated in a comprehensive survey conducted by *BOMA* (The Building Owners and Managers Association) and *ULI* (The Urban Land Institute). The survey was designed to determine what tenants think are the most important features, amenities, and services in their office buildings.

The results, published in a report entitled *What Office Tenants Want,* offer revealing, current, detailed data about what tenants value most as occupiers of office space. By practicing strategic customer service, managers will win dissatisfied tenants from the competition and secure the longevity of their own current tenants. This "Tenant Wish List" represents a "Priorities List" for property management.

TENANT ATTITUDES ABOUT BUILDING FEATURES, AMENITIES, SERVICES

Feature, Amenity or Service	Important (%)	Satisfied (%)
Rental rates (incl. pass-throughs/escalations)	99	88
Comfort temperature	99	74
Indoor air quality	99	81
Acoustic/noise control	99	83
Building management's ability to meet your need	99	89
Quality of building maintenance work	99	89
Building management's responsiveness	99	86
Effectiveness of communications	99	93
Appearance of building	98	92

(**Source**: *BOMA/ULI Survey*)

The numbers in the first column represent the percentage of respondents to whom a particular feature is important. The second column represents the percentage of those respondents who were satisfied with that particular service/feature/amenity.

The Importance of Building Management & Services

In the same *BOMA/ULI* Survey, tenants also rated the relative importance of building management to their satisfaction with each of the following aspects of building management and services:

- **Building management's responsiveness**
- **Quality of building maintenance work**
- **Building management's ability to meet tenants' needs**
- **Effectiveness of communications with building management**

Building Management's Ability to Meet Tenant's Needs:

Tenant Responses:	1%	Not Important
	7%	Important
	92%	Very Important

Quality Maintenance Work:

Tenant Responses:	1%	Not Important
	6%	Important
	93%	Very Important

Building Management's Responsiveness:

Tenant Responses:	1%	Not Important
	7%	Important
	92%	Very Important

Building Management's Responsiveness with Building Management:

Tenant Responses:	1%	Not Important
	11%	Important
	83%	Very Important

Survey results highlight the importance of building management's efforts to provide and sustain effective communication with clients and clearly demonstrate that providing quality building management services is imperative to customer satisfaction.

The alternative can be a costly endeavor, as is demonstrated in our segment on the Cost of Poor Service.

The Cost of Poor Service

A look at the cost of poor service illustrates the value of consistent, reliable customer care. As many as one customer in four is dissatisfied enough to start doing business with the competition. Of those customers, only 5% will actually register a complaint; the other 95% prefer to switch rather than fight.

In short, at any point, 25% of any business is undependable.

"It is important to understand that the total existence of a company depends upon the customer, so if the customer is not satisfied, he is not going to be a customer tomorrow, and if he is not a customer tomorrow, we don't have a business tomorrow."

—*Harvey Lamm, President of Subaru of America*

---

15 Residuals of Poor Service

Poor service comes in many shapes, sizes, and attitudes. A snide remark in the presence of a client. Sloppy workmanship. A heated Email.

So what exactly IS poor service? What does it look like? How do I spot it when I see it? In essence, there are fifteen qualities of poor service for you to look for, improve upon, and eliminate altogether:

- Laziness

- Personality

- Poor Choice of Words

- Broken Promises

- Empty Promises

- Poor Workmanship

- Ego

- Untidy Appearance
- Sloppiness
- Disheveled Uniform
- Laziness
- Threats
- Fixing the Wrong Thing
- Not Fixing the Right Thing
- Not Fixing *Anything*

The Cost of Negative Customer Experiences

According to one landmark study conducted by the Technical Assistance Research Programs Institute of Washington, D.C., the average dissatisfied customer tells eight to ten other people about his or her ordeal—even if the complaint is resolved satisfactorily. The study also reveals that it takes twelve positive experiences to correct a single bad one. (See "Complaint Management" for more on this topic.)

COST OF POOR SERVICE

Property:	ABC Building
Size:	225,000 sq. ft.

Total number of tenants in the property	34
Percentage of dissatisfied tenants	.25
Number of dissatisfied tenants	9
Percentage of dissatisfied tenants apt to move	.70
Number of dissatisfied tenants who are apt to move	6

Average annual revenue per
tenant @ 6,600 sq. ft. x $12.00/sq. ft.　　=　$79,200.00

Annual revenue at risk because of poor service　=　$475,200.00

The loss of six tenants at ABC Building represents nearly half a million dollars in lost rent; almost one-fifth of the total gross potential income is at risk because of poor service.

At this price, what business can afford NOT to provide excellent service?

9 Ways Poor Customer Service Can Come Back to Haunt You

In the same study cited previously, it was found that the average dissatisfied customer tells **eight** to **ten** other people about his or her ordeal—even if the complaint is resolved satisfactorily. The study also reveals that *it takes twelve positive experiences to correct a single bad one.*

Using the figures from the ABC Building, the following is a demonstration of the cost of negative word-of-mouth:

COST OF NEGATIVE CUSTOMER EXPERIENCE

Number of dissatisfied tenants apt to move	6
Number of potential tenants who will hear about poor service and rent elsewhere (6 x 8)	48

Potential lost revenue opportunity to ABC Building Dollars at risk because of negative word-of-mouth is
$3,801,600.00

Once a tenant is lost, chances are they are lost for good. So is the opportunity for a satisfied tenant to spread *good* word of mouth. Instead, you are left with an unsatisfied tenant who is more than likely spreading *bad* word of mouth. Here are ten ways negative word of mouth can come back to haunt you:

- Loss of *one* dissatisfied client
- Loss of a future dissatisfied client
- Loss of a future prospective client
- Dissatisfaction of a current client
- Complaints by a current client
- An atmosphere of distrust in the building
- Loss of credibility in the professional community
- Loss of respect by professional peers
- Loss of another testimonial by a satisfied client

4 Steps for Providing Quality Service

The key to developing the highest possible service standards is first organizing the process into bite-sized pieces. There are four steps for accomplishing this heroic feat:

- **Define Your "Service Sequences":** A service sequence is to your business what chapters are to a book. They are a way of conveniently subdividing the aspects of your service so that you can discover the specific customer encounters that need standards. View your service sequences from your customers' perspective. If they looked at your business as separate chunks, what would they see?

- **Map out the Steps:** After you break your business up into its various chapters, choose one area that needs improvement (as indicated by customer feedback or other research). Next, map out the major chronological steps that make up that particular customer encounter (like the paragraphs within a chapter).

- **Supercharging Satisfaction:** For each individual step, ask yourself: What general service qualities will supercharge the customer's satisfaction of doing business with my company during this step? Carry out this same procedure for each step until you have determined each step's key experience-enhancing qualities, then use them to supercharge customer satisfaction.

- **Convert your satisfaction superchargers into "standards."** Finally, rewrite the step-by-step interaction by converting your general service qualities into your specific service standards.

10 Unseen Benefits of Quality Service

Quality customer service has numerous benefits, many of them unseen. To keep you focused on the goal of quality customer service, each and every time, here are the top ten:

- Satisfied customers
- Future customers
- Happy tenants
- Professional credibility
- Positive word of mouth
- Glowing testimonials
- Good buzz
- Company pride
- Self pride
- Truth in advertising

10 Ways to Win Customer Loyalty

Quality is defined by the desires and needs of the client. Loyal tenants are the most valuable resource of *any* business—and especially commercial real estate. Quality customer service begins the moment contact is made and is an on-going practice of every member of your organization. Here are 10 ways to win customer loyalty:

- Develop a customer-driven rather than financial-driven policy
- Understand that the benefits of customer service outweigh the cost
- Make customer service a company obsession
- Make sure all staff understand the Corporate Mission
- Convey your service strategy to all front-line staff
- Publish your service standards
- Demand that all staff members are customer-oriented
- Make sure that staff members take the *time* to serve
- Make sure that employees know customer service is *their* concern, not someone else's
- Ensure that recovery is immediate and superlative

The Five Dimensions of Quality Service

There are five true dimensions of quality service that should be kept in mind while preparing your own company's unique service standards. They are as follows:

- **Reliability.** The ability to perform the promised service dependably and accurately. This ensures a trouble-free occupancy that offers value-added services and maintains service standards.

- **Tangibles.** The appearance of physical facilities, equipment, personnel, and communications material. These include the parking lot, landscaping, cleanliness, and quality of occupied space.

- **Responsiveness.** The willingness of your staff to help customers and to provide prompt service. This ensures that a fully empowered front-line staff *promptly* and *effectively* handles complaints with *courtesy*.

- **Assurance.** The knowledge and courtesy of employees and their ability to convey trust and confidence: publish service standards, communicate with customers, and conduct satisfaction surveys.

- **Empathy.** The provision of caring, individualized attention to tenants. Make sure property managers greet customers by name and ask how they want to be served.

Do It Right The First Time!

Strong leaders who set high service standards nurture a "do-it-right-the-first-time" culture. As we have shown throughout this section, you may not get a second chance to "make things right," so it naturally behooves you do "get it right" the first time—and every subsequent time.

"When a company performs a service carelessly, when it makes avoidable mistakes and fails to deliver on the alluring promises made to attract customers, it shakes the customers' confidence in its capabilities and undermines its chances of earning a reputation for service excellence."

—**Berry Parasuraman**, *Marketing Services*

---

6 Reasons to "Get it Right the First Time"

There are many reasons for getting it right the first time. Getting it right the first time:

- **Improves market effectiveness**. When excellence is your service standard, you are more able to achieve it on a consistent basis. Begin by getting it right the first time, and you'll get it right *every* time!

- **Increases retention rates**. Getting the tenant is only half the battle; keeping them is an ongoing struggle. Getting it right the first time ensures that tenants feel more assured of staying, and less inclined to leave.

- **Leads to repeat business**. Customer service is a national obsession. From fast-food chains to movie clerks, the level of service they receive rarely satisfies customers. Getting it right the first time will lead to repeat business by making you a standout in a field of not even close.

- **Results in positive word of mouth**. Word of mouth, especially *positive* word of mouth, is the gift that keeps on giving. There is no telling what word of mouth can do for your new—and repeat—business, and no way to measure it. The only goal is to foster it. How? By getting it right the first time . . .

- **Increases ability to command premium price**. Premium is a label that is hard to live up to these days. Many promise it, few deliver. By getting it right the first time, you will be proving that you are worth the premium price you demand.

- **Promotes brand awareness**. Nothing shouts branding more loudly—or more clearly—than getting it right the first time. Your brand is only as strong as your last mistake, so not making any should only increase the strength of your brand ten-fold.

5 Benefits of Getting it Right the First Time

You've seen *how* to get it right the first time, but how about *why*? There are five benefits to getting it right the first time. They are as follows:

- Happy Clients
- Personal Pride
- A Standard of Quality That is Easy to Duplicate
- Glowing Testimonials
- Positive Word of Mouth

Recognizing Elements of Customer Service:
Developing Service Standards

> "It is critical that the Chief Executive Officer is the number one champion of the customer."
>
> —**Donald R. Libey**

In developing service standards for your organization, it is important to differentiate between Pre-Sale Service Standards, Occupancy Standards, and After-Sale Standards. What follows is a discussion of each:

6 Strategies for Achieving Pre-Sale Service Standards

What strategies will ensure pre-sale customer satisfaction? Service, once delivered, is a tangible product that can be measured, assessed, and valued. Service begins at the moment of first contact in the pre-sales process. Here are six strategies for achieving quality pre-sale service standards:

- **Marketing:** Informative, targeted, and focused.

- **Verbal Response:** Attentive, interested, and timely.

- **Communication:** Conveys a clear understanding of the customer's needs.

- **Purchase Environment:** Welcoming and non-threatening environment designed to help customers feel comfortable.

- **Staff:** Responsive, knowledgeable, empathetic, empowered employees whose personal appearance meets customer expectations.

- **Documentation:** Compressed, concise, and accurate.

5 Strategies for Achieving Occupancy Standards

Client satisfaction—and customer retention—relies on the following five specific occupancy standards:

- **Consistent delivery of promised service**: On time, *every* time.

- **Lifetime of "zero defects"**: 100% customer satisfaction, *every* time.

- **Matching reality with expectations**: Don't promise the moon if you can only give them the stars.

- **Giving greater value than the cost of the purchase**: Don't give them what they pay for, give them *more* than what they pay for.

- **Giving satisfaction in excess of expectations**: Exceeding customer's expectations on a consistent and reliable basis, not just during "the honeymoon phase."

3 Strategies for Achieving After-Sales Standards

As previous sections have discussed, the sale is only the beginning of a long and hopefully prosperous working relationship. To achieve this end, there are three specific strategies for achieving high after-sales standards:

- **Maintained Interest:** Frequent contact with tenant—maintaining the long-term relationship and anticipating future needs

- **Complaint Handling:** Empowered staff responding immediately, courteously, honestly, and thoroughly, keeping the customer advised throughout the process.

- **Measurement:** Consistently evaluating the level of service provided and assessing customer satisfaction through surveys.

Structuring for Service Excellence

Most companies do not become service leaders through blind evolution. Becoming a service leader takes more than good management. It calls for making profound changes in the way you operate and manage, including adapting the four basic elements of service:

- **Service Strategy**
- **Leadership**
- **Empowerment**
- **Measurement**

4 Steps to Seamless Service Strategy

The first and most important step toward outstanding service is developing a Service Strategy. Service Strategy sets the stage and defines all other activities for delivering excellent customer service. In order to design a successful service strategy, managers should take the following steps:

- **Decide on organizational goals**
- **Be willing to pay the short-term cost**
- **Appeal to highly motivated people**
- **Listen to what others are saying**

The goal of the service strategy is to position the organization and promote a culture of excellence.

3 Aims of a Successful Service Strategy

An effective service strategy should not exist in a vacuum. It should not be full of grand schemes and unreachable dreams. Effective service strategy is a non-trivial statement of intent that:

- Noticeably **differentiates** you from others
- Has **value** in the eyes of customers and employees
- Is **deliverable** by the organization

3 Components of a Successful Service Strategy

There are three components of a successful service strategy. These components define behavior, bond team members, and motivate individuals throughout the organization. They comprise a set of principles for improving and delivering consistent, quality customer service. The three components essential to successful adaptation of the service strategy are:

- **Mission Statement**
- **Attitude Shift**
- **Value Disciplines**

Component #1: *The Mission Statement*

A critical and initial key element of the Service Strategy is the establishment of a Mission Statement, such as the example given below:

*The Associates, Partners, and Staff of **ABC Corporation** will strive to be the finest Commercial Real Estate Service Provider in the nation, providing unparalleled, customized service and attention to detail.*

The establishment of a Mission Statement synthesizes the company. It affects subsequent plans and decision, coloring the whole organization, from its culture to its public image.

5 Traits of an Effective Mission Statement

Writing a mission statement is the easy part; *living* it is much more difficult. In order to make your own mission statement less dreamy, and more livable, here are the five successful traits of an effective mission statement:

- **Conceivable**: Start by realizing what it is you *want* to do. Then try to do it, using your mission statement as a tool.

- **Believable**: Will tenants believe your mission statement? If not, why not? Is it full of hot air? If so, let some out!

- **Achievable**: Your mission statement must be realistic, above all else. This does not mean to limit yourself, but instead to *know* yourself. Recognize your weaknesses, as well as your strengths. Remember that you can always rewrite a mission statement later.

- **Doable**: Is it realistic? Can you actually do it, every day, every month, every year? If not, it's back to the drawing board until you can.

- **Livable**: Can you live with your mission statement? Is it something that can be passed down for generations and stand the test of time? Your standards should be high enough to achieve, but not so high as to deceive—yourselves.

Component #2: *Attitude Shift*

Successful adaptation of the service strategy often requires building a new service-oriented culture—requiring a complete attitude shift—from the top down. Unless there is an overriding commitment to customer service throughout the *entire* organization, the actual service provided will be mediocre, at best.

In order to develop, promote, and achieve consistent levels of excellent service, the following ten essential attitudinal shifts should create the culture of the organization:

10 Essential Attitudinal Shifts

A shift in attitude from poor customer service to excellent customer service is essential. But how? Here are ten essential attitudinal shifts, consisting of an ineffective *before* and a very effective *after*:

FROM:	TO:
Being Good	Being *Excellent*
Quality of Space	Quality of *Everything*
Management Support	Management *Involvement*
Function Isolation	Team Energy
Quality is Someone Else's Concern	Quality is *MY* Concern
Some Employees Have Customers	All Employees Have Customers
Recovery is a Problem	Recovery is an *Opportunity*
Errors are Inevitable	Doing it Right *Every* Time
Service is Shapeless	Service is Seamless
Quality-improvement Programs	Continuous Improvement

15 Words to Foster a Positive Attitude

Having a hard time creating a positive attitudinal shift in your organization, or perhaps personally? Sometimes a word is worth a thousand smiles. Even better, here are fifteen words designed to foster a positive attitude:

- Great
- Super
- Fantastic
- Superb
- Splendid
- Sensational
- Marvelous
- Wonderful
- Smashing
- Outstanding
- Terrific
- Far-out
- Excellent
- Superb
- Over-and-Above

Component #3: *Value Disciplines*

At the heart of the service strategy is a set of core value disciplines that will make or break your company's ability to create unsurpassed value at a profit. As their name implies, these *disciplines* do not come easily. They must be molded through daily practice and strong, vocal leadership . . .

> "If you want loyalty, you have to look after your customers. And to do that you have to look after your staff, because they are not going to give great service unless they want to."
>
> —**Julian Richer**, *Richer Sounds*

4 Key Value Disciplines

Basic, consistent values that can be displayed through actions allow consumers to consistently choose a company built on strong foundations rather than a company with an unclear mission and uncertain goal. The four key value disciplines are:

- **Operational Excellence**: Providing customers with consistent, reliable, seamless service at competitive prices, delivered with minimal difficulty or inconvenience.

- **Product Leadership**: Providing product/services that continually redefine the state of the art. Thinking ahead of the curve.

- **Customer Intimacy**: A pro-active approach to customer service. Anticipating customer needs. Selling the customer a total solution, not just a product or service.

- **Leadership**: Leadership makes the Service Strategy an everyday reality. Successful providers of service depend on managers who are completely and fanatically committed to excellent customer service.

7 Responsibilities of the Senior Manager

What is the senior manager's responsibility in all of this? There are seven major duties of the senior manager in creating value disciplines. They are as follows:

- Be approachable, available, and attentive
- Identify relationship problems before they affect customer care
- Understand that a culture based on the internal customer will reinforce a drive to satisfy external customers
- Share information and resources
- Communicate frequently
- Provide constructive feedback
- Publicly reward excellence

4 Reasons Why Leadership Matters

If customer service has to extend throughout the company or organization, from top to bottom, do you really need leadership? The answer is a resounding "yes." Leadership matters for the four following reasons:

- **Discretion:** Leadership matters because service providers must rely on discretion when serving customers.

- **An Established Service Culture:** Employees have to rely on, and trust in, the service culture to guide them in making decisions. This can't exist without strong leadership.

- **Teamwork:** Customer service has to be all-inclusive, throughout the company or organization. Service leaders take great pains to hire service-oriented personnel whom they then train to become real estate practitioners, giving each other a team to rely on.

- **Leading by Example:** You cannot train a personality to serve; some people simply do not like to serve others. In this case, strong leadership must teach customer service not by training, but by *example*!

The Importance of Empowerment

Empowering employees gives them the freedom to act. While a company's dedication to excellent customer service is paramount, if a company is to survive, each employee's ability to manage the inevitable complaints and to provide solutions must be an essential element of customer service. They must have the *freedom*—to *act*.

To really succeed, the pursuit of excellence in customer service must become an undying obsession. It requires every single person in the organization to focus their energies and their enthusiasm not just on getting it right, but *improving* it. For this, they must feel *empowered* . . .

8 Ways to Empower Front-line Staff

In order to provide excellent service, employees must think, decide, and act proactively and intelligently according to their perception of the good of the customers and the company. This vital component of *empowerment* must not be left to chance. Empowerment changes people's relationship with the company; it becomes "our" company instead of "their" company. Here are eight ways to empower front-line staff:

- **Lead by Example**: Demonstrate service excellence though your actions.

- **Build Confidence**: Explain the Service Strategy.

- **Motivate**: Convey the concept that every employee has customers.

- **Foster Commitment**: Have front-line staff help develop service standards.

- **Empower**: Give staff the authority to act for the customer.

- **Standardize**: Provide guidelines for service recovery.

- **Train**: Provide employees with appropriate skills, systems and customer service training.

- **Reward Excellence**: Provide incentives; develop goals—together.

20 Empowering Words

Empowerment does not occur by osmosis. It is an active process that works from the top down, on a daily basis, in every area of the operation. Here are twenty words to help you empower your staff, your employees, or perhaps even—yourself:

- Trust
- Faith
- Loyalty
- Belief
- Confidence
- Devotion
- Allegiance
- Fidelity
- Reliance
- Dependence

- Responsibility
- Future
- Togetherness
- Belief
- Entrust
- Sureness
- Assurance
- Certainty
- Ownership
- Security

2 Ways to Facilitate Excellent Customer Service

Without empowerment, employees and coworkers are often left to wonder "how someone else would do this?" But as we have shown, they must learn "how *they* should do this…" Indifference and inaction often reflect lack of understanding and lack of communication about service strategy. Facilitate excellent customer service by:

- **Widening the solution boundaries for employees.**
- **Sustaining on-going practice of an effective Service Strategy.**

4 Ways to Create a Customer-centered Atmosphere

Becoming service-oriented is a process, not an event. How can managers create an atmosphere of customer-centered service among their employees? Here are four ways to start:

- When an employee does not know what to do— **COMMUNICATE**.

- When an employee does not know how to do it—**TRAIN**.

- When an employee is energized and wants to participate— **EMPOWER**.

- When an employee does not want to do it—**MOTIVATE**.

10 Customer-centered Words

Occasionally the word "customer" gets used so often in a conversation—get the customer this, the customer wants that, customer service—that it loses its very meaning. To avoid that problem, here are twelve words to help you put the customer first, each and every time, even in your conversation:

- Consumer
- Buyer
- Prospect
- Tenant
- Potential Buyer
- Client
- Purchaser
- Shopper
- Patron
- Purchasing Agent

Measurement

Quality is defined by the customer's perception. Successful companies survey their customers frequently. Tenant retention is the *measurement* of the commercial property manager's success. So, how do you "measure" up?

7 Ways to Measure Client Satisfaction

It is vital to understand what factors sway tenants in favor of renewing their lease, particularly those factors that are within *your* control. Certainly costs, inducements, and amenities are all major considerations. However, office tenants also place a high value on quality management of the building. Here are seven ways to measure tenant satisfaction, and the frequency in which you should engage in their measurement:

Method:	Frequency:
Customer complaint solicitation	Continuous
Post-transaction follow-up surveys	Continuous
Managers call customers for feedback	Weekly
Customer focus groups	Monthly
"Mystery shopping" of service providers	Quarterly
Employee surveys	Quarterly
Total market service quality survey	Annually

21 Measurement Related Words

Anytime the aspect of measurement comes up, an entire list of terminology is soon to follow. To vary your use of language in your forms of measurement, especially those a prospect, tenant, or client might see, here is a list of twenty-one measurement related words to interchange in both documentation and speech:

- Assessment
- Estimation
- Determination
- Appraisal
- Calculation
- Evaluation
- Analysis
- Computation
- Judgement
- Dimensions
- Area
- Proportion
- Size
- Extent
- Magnitude
- Scope
- Range
- Foot
- Inch
- Yard
- Specifications

8 Goals of Customer Satisfaction Surveys

The commitment to excellent service cannot be taken lightly. In making this commitment, management must continuously evaluate and measure performance levels and customer satisfaction, and then must be prepared to act where and when necessary if goals and service levels are not being met—or maintained. This task can often be accomplished through "client satisfaction surveys." Here are eight goals of such surveys:

- Responsiveness and follow-through
- Appearance and condition of the property
- Quality of management services
- Quality of the leasing services
- Tenant relations
- Renewal information
- Property characteristics
- Readiness to solve problems

17 Rewards for Taking a Survey

Ask any marketing rep and they'll tell you: Nowadays, people expect something in return for taking a survey. After all, they're time consuming, labor intensive, and usually benefit anyone else other than the survey taker. To provide the most prompt and objective survey results in your building, here is a sampling of seventeen simple and inexpensive rewards one might offer for taking a survey:

- Key-chain
- Magnet
- Frame

- Office supply of some sort
- Pen
- Stationary
- FREE service of some kind
- Coupon
- Candy
- Snack foods
- Paperweight
- Calendar
- Bookmark
- Stress ball
- Photo cube
- Desk blotter

6 Measurement Criteria for Tenant/Customer Satisfaction

In addition to surveying your customers, tenants, clients, and employees, the following services and processes should be continuously measured and evaluated within the organization:

- **Response Times**: How long does it take from the time the customer calls in a complaint until the complaint is successfully resolved?

- **Service Calls & Maintenance**: Follow-up when service calls or special requests are made. For example: Was the repair successfully completed? Is the customer happy with the repair? Or, did the customer receive the information requested? Was it useful/helpful?

- **Leasing Activity**: Measure time from lease signing to occupancy.

- **Move-in**: Survey customer the following day and ask for feedback regarding the move.

- **Building Tours**: Measure and monitor follow-up activity on all customers who took a building tour.

- **Attitude of all Service Team Members**: Test the service; go on a "mystery shopping spree."

2 Benefits of Measurement Criteria

Measuring the level of service your company is providing completes the service cycle. Managers that take customer satisfaction seriously constantly assess their performance against process, product, and satisfaction. Asking these questions frequently, and carefully analyzing the data collected, will enable managers to:

- **Build a Service Quality Information System**
- **Measure the system that delivers the service**

7 Steps to Designing a Survey

Surveying your customers is one of the best indicators of current—and future—success. But what belongs in a customer satisfaction survey? The following considerations are of paramount importance when designing measurement surveys:

- The survey should take only 10-12 minutes to complete
- Limit number of questions to 45-50
- Keep questions short and concise
- Avoid open-ended questions
- Never ask negative questions
- Never ask questions you can't resolve
- Develop a 6-point grading scale

8 Forms of Presenting a Survey

How you present a survey is often critical in how many you get back, how quickly you get them back, and even how objective they are. Surveys that are difficult to read, require additional postage, or otherwise unwieldy are often both ineffective and negative. To avoid being either, here are eight alternative ways of presenting a survey that are designed with your tenant in mind:

- Email form (NOT an attachment)
- Checklist on a colored flyer
- Suggestion card
- Weekly quiz on postcard
- Suggestion box
- (Quick) Phone survey
- Handouts in break room with accompanying return box
- Postcard form with prepaid postage

Offering Value Added Services

Don't make customer service a losing proposition. Make it beneficial for all parties involved. Value added services are business products, services, and conveniences designed to enhance the level of customer service provided, brand the type of service provided, and in many cases generate additional revenue. Fees from value added services can be leveraged to increase revenue up to $1/sq.ft.

30 Value Added Occupancy Services to Offer

It is well known that creating real estate solutions to meet a tenant's broader business needs helps tenants conduct business productively, efficiently, and economically. State-of-the-art properties offer value added amenities such as restaurants, health clubs, banks, child care centers, and valet services—all designed to meet the needs of a more sophisticated tenant seeking to retain their employees by improving their work environment. Here is a list of thirty such occupancy services:

- Clothing Sales
- Tailoring
- Fitness Center
- Internet Services
- Video Conferencing
- Multi-Media Booth
- Cable TV Access
- Copying & Printing Services
- Laundry Services
- Shoe Shine & Repair
- Meal delivery

- Daycare Facilities
- Car Wash & Detail Service
- Valet Parking
- Pharmacy Delivery
- Concierge Services
- Courier Service
- Beauty Parlor
- Floral Delivery
- Postal Services
- Magazine Stand
- Snack Bar
- Game Room
- Designated Smoking Area
- Sidewalks (for walking during breaks)
- Attractive Break Rooms
- Convenient Access to Mass Transit
- Vending Machines
- Lobby Receptionist
- Security System

Michael J. Lipsey

The 3-Point System for Determining What Services to Offer

Knowing what services are available to offer is one thing, but what do you do with such information? After all, each new tenant brings along a new list of needs and requirements. Determining what services to offer each and every one of your tenants is an ongoing process that begins with the following three steps:

- **Focus Groups:** The first step in providing value-added services for your tenants is to hold focus groups with strategic representative tenants and determine an overview of the services that should be offered.

- **Surveys:** Next, survey all tenants to determine what needs are not being met, what services are merely on a tenant's wish list, and what services would make life easier for your tenants.

- **Feedback:** According to the results of the research conducted, a list of services to be offered should be developed, devised, and implemented.

Sample Survey: *Tenant Service Needs*

In a further effort to determine exactly what your tenants want, here is a sample survey for your tenant's service needs:

1. Check each of the following services that you use at least once a week.

___ Food services	___ Medical Station/Healthcare
___ Copy Center	___ Health Club Facilities
___ Daycare	___ Car Detail/gas
___ Dry Cleaning	___ Travel Agency
___ Construction Management	___ Space Planning
___ Office Services (copying, etc.)	___ Conference Facilities
___ Training Rooms	___ Video Conferencing Rentals
___ Renting Lobby for events	___ Florist
___ Concierge Services	___ Car Rental
___ Kiosks	___ Other (please list)

2. Please estimate how much time you spend, including travel, to attain the services listed above per week? _____

3. If the services listed above were available within the office building, would you rather purchase the products and services on-site?
   A. Yes
   B. No

4. Gender ___ Male ___ Female

5. How many individuals work in your office location? _____

"The idea of having access to any service or facility you might need and only paying for it when you use it is fundamental to the commercial ethos of the building. There is no better way to respond to the realities of the market."

—**Paul Storey**, *Property Director for the International Financial Center, London*

Setting Standards and Keeping the Service Promise

All declarations of intent made by the organization, corporately or individually, are perceived by the customers as promises—and *must be met*. Companies win business by promising service; they retain business by *keeping* this promise.

For example:

- They promise to deliver within seven days—and do so.
- They promise to reply within two days—and do so.
- They promise to call back this afternoon—and do so.
- They promise to repair a fault within 24 hours—and do so.

Delivering reliable service consistently requires that management establish standards and best practices throughout the organization designed to streamline service delivered. The following section is designed to show you how to do just that . . .

17 Words to Use Instead of "Promise"

So many promises get broken in the course of working with our customers that it can often take on a negative connotation in a tenant's mind. To avoid this unconscious roadblock, here are seventeen similar words to use in place of promise in your printed documents and speech:

- Pledge
- Agreement
- Covenant
- Engagement

- Guarantee
- Assurance
- Vow
- Pact
- Warrant
- Voucher
- Contract
- Arrangement
- Understanding
- Transaction
- Bargain
- Bond
- Treaty

Michael J. Lipsey

9 Customer Service Standards

Where to begin? Simple: The *customer*. All customers are entitled to the nine following service standards:

- Fair, courteous, and professional treatment.
- Information that is accurate and current.
- Timely responses to requests.
- Reasonable access to appropriate staff.
- Confidence in the appropriate staff to do the job right.
- Two-way communication between tenant and staff.
- Opportunities for collaboration and partnerships, as appropriate.
- Participation in the company's decision-making process.
- Consideration of their opinions and concerns by the company.

Benefits of Service Standards

Realistic and well-thought-out service standards provide a practical way to manage performance in an era of fiscal restraint and help shape the expectations tenants bring with them with their office equipment. Experience suggests that services can be improved and delivered at reduced cost by conveying the following five benefits of service standards:

- Refocusing services on tenants.
- Finding out what tenants consider to be critical aspects of services and their delivery.
- Giving managers the flexibility to respond to tenant needs.
- Developing proper incentives to promote innovation.
- Monitoring and analyzing performance against realistic goals and standards.

4 Things Service Standards do for Tenants

What does a tenant get from effective service standards? As an integral part of good management, service standards:

- Promote partnership in quality customer service.

- Provide the means to measure service performance and costs reliably.

- Provide meaningful information on the content, value, and method of service delivery.

- Use performance and customer satisfaction information to guide operational decisions to improve service standards and actual performance continually.

Michael J. Lipsey

15 Steps to Implementing *Realistic* Service Standards

Service standards are a lot like potholders: they're only helpful if you actually *use* them! To ensure that you are implementing *realistic* service standards—those you and your tenants can actually benefit from—here are fifteen sensible steps to take first:

- Identify direct and indirect customers.

- Identify services.

- Identify partners (for joint performance agreements in service delivery)

- Define your current activities.

- Know what is affordable: What does it cost to deliver your proposed services?

- Establish standards to which customers can relate.

- Consider piloting a standard on a small scale, and provide cost projections when appropriate and reasonable.

- Fine-tune the standard.

- Define performance measures.

- Set up and articulate a performance measurement strategy.

- Train and equip staff to help customers, and let staff know what is expected of them.

- Empower front-line staff to make decisions.

- Train managers and supervisors in leadership and motivation.

- Advise staff and customers of service standards.

- Report on performance you provide vs. standards.

5 Questions to Ask Your Tenants Before Setting Standards

When establishing fair and mutually beneficial service standards, why not go right to the source? Here are five great questions to ask your tenants:

- What are the most important features of the service we provide?
- What is your satisfaction level with this service?
- What changes do you need or want?
- What are your expectations?
- What do you perceive are *your* responsibilities?

10 Ways to Ensure Customer Loyalty

Is it really true that the days of "loyal" customers are finally over? Not if you implement the following ten ways to ensure customer loyalty, they're not:

- Company has customer-driven rather than financial-driven policy
- Company understands that the benefits of customer service outweigh costs
- Customer Service is an obsession practiced by every member of the firm
- All staff members understand the Corporate Mission and Vision
- Company conveys Service Strategy to front-line staff and explains their role in its successful delivery
- Service Standards are published
- All staff members are trained in the delivery of excellent Customer Service
- Staff members are responsive and take the time to serve
- All employees accept responsibility for the delivery of excellent Customer Service

8 Criteria for Effective Service Standards

Service standards can serve two purposes:

1. They are a powerful way of shaping the image that your customers have of you;

2. They are a great management tool for measuring how well each person in your company meets the levels of service to which you aspire. Too few companies have meaningful standards because they do not know how to translate a *general* service "quality" into a *specific* service "standard." General service qualities can be defined by adjectives that describe the basic ways you want your staff (and managers) to treat your customers, including:

- Caring
- Courteous
- Efficient
- Friendly
- Helpful
- Pleasant
- Prompt
- Responsive

Service Reliability

In a recent survey, customers stated they would pay more than 12% more for better quality and 9% more for better service. Service Reliability also improves operating efficiencies by reducing the need for re-performing the service, increasing productivity, raising employee morale, and lowering employee turnover.

Service flaws, such as a repairman's failure to show up at the scheduled time is an example of a service flaw that occurs in the presence of the customer. Therefore, performing service right the first time involves a great sense of immediacy and a greater degree of discipline.

The Service Reliability Test

The complexity of service reliability poses unique challenges and requires the establishment of standards from which the service can be measured. Before becoming completely satisfied with your current level of service reliability, ask yourself the following questions:

1. Is your goal zero service errors in maintenance requests? Lease calculations? Lease negotiation? (When have you achieved that goal?)

2. Do you have a grasp of the inefficiencies of your current system? (Have you preformed an audit on error-prone areas?)

3. Are you communicating your commitment? (Name three ways you communicate commitment to your tenants and tenants.)

4. Have you adequately prepared? (What resources do you have that contribute to performance reliability?)

5. Have you built a continually improving process? (Name two improvements in the last quarter.)

Service Quality vs. Service Standard

The most important element of the service standard is that it is conveyed to all parties—the employees as well as the tenant. Only then does the standard become a measure of expectation. But what is the difference between a service *quality* and a service **standard**? Here are two examples that clearly define the pros and cons of both:

- Service *Quality* might mean answering the telephone promptly.

- Service **Standard** means answering the telephone within three rings.

- Service *Quality* means being responsive to the customer

- Service **Standard** means responding to and/or repairing all service requests within 24 hours.

6 General Service Qualities vs. Specific Service Standards

The following table lists some examples of how general service qualities can be turned into specific service standards. The measurable aspect of each standard is in bold type:

Service Quality	Service Standard
Answer the phone promptly.	Answer the phone **within three rings**.
Return customer calls in a timely fashion.	Return all customer calls **within 24 hours**.
Be attentive to the customer.	Make eye contact with the customer **within 5 seconds of their approaching you**.
Be empathetic with an upset customer.	Always **apologize** if a customer is upset.
Take personal responsibility for helping the customer	Always give the customer **your name, phone number, and extension**.
Dress appropriately for work.	Wear your business "uniform" **at all times**.

6 Traits of Service Standards

To better exemplify the definition of a true service standard, here are six traits of what a service standard requires:

- **Specific**: Lofty visions and utopia have no place in a service standard. True service standards are specific and targeted toward the tenant and his or her particular needs.

- **Concise**: Short and to the point. So go the best service standards which use complete sentences to portray specific steps.

- **Measurable**: How do we *measure* this standard? Not philosophically, but physically? Keep asking yourself this question as you form your own. Why? You can bet that the tenant is asking it as well!

- **Based on tenant wants**: A true service standard is not based on what you think a tenant wants, but rather on what a tenant really wants, discovered through the various means of research we've discussed.

- **Part of job descriptions**: A service standard must be part of the everyday operation of a company, just like clocking in and clocking out.

- **Created as a team:** Though front-line employees may have more to say about a standard than others, a true service standard is created by a team working together, always mindful of the *customer* first.

The 7 Criteria of an Effective Service Standard

We've seen how you can measure a service standard, but what makes the standard itself effective? Seven criteria make a service standard effective. It should be:

- **Specific:** Standards tell service people precisely and exactly what is expected of them. They do not have to guess about your expectations or make anything up.

- **Concise:** Standards do not explain the philosophy behind the action. Instead, they go right to the point and spell out who should do what by when.

- **Measurable:** Because the actions in a standard are all specific criteria, they are observable and objective, which makes them easy to quantify.

- **Based on customer requirements:** Standards should be based on customer requirements and not just your industry's standards. Fulfilling your customers' expectations gives you an advantage over your competitors.

- **Written into job descriptions and performance reviews:** If you want employees to adhere to the standards, then write them down and make them part of each employee's job description and performance review. Using standards as a management tool gives them more credibility.

- **Jointly created with staff:** The best standards are created by management and staff together based on their mutual understanding of customer needs. You may want to consider using focus groups as a vehicle for having staff come up with service standards.

- **Fairly enforced:** Standards that are enforced with some people and not with others quickly erode. Company-wide standards require that everybody, including the top brass, conform to them. Department-specific standards apply to everyone within that department, including the manager.

5 Sources to Solicit for Service Standards

Service quality and standards are applicable to all staff who come in contact with the customer, regardless of department, division, or station. When developing service standards, solicit input from employees actually performing the service, including:

- **Building Maintenance**
- **Building Engineers**
- **Property Managers**
- **Leasing Agents**
- **Outside Contractors**

4 Ways to Measure Smiles

Service standards go one step further by turning general service qualities into specific, measurable *actions* that you expect your staff to take in given situations. In order for your staff to understand what you mean by friendly service, you must break the definition down into the components that make up "friendly." By taking these observable actions, your staff conveys friendliness to your customers:

- Smile at customers as they approach.
- Make direct eye contact while explaining the situation.
- Greet customers with "Good morning" or "Good afternoon."
- Use the customer's name at least twice during the conversation.

9 Steps for Continued Improvement

In addition to monitoring service standards and service delivery, it is also essential to assess service on a larger scale. Continuous improvement requires ongoing assessment of both the results of performance monitoring, such as tenant and employee satisfaction, and the manner in which performance is monitored. Some examples of activities which lead to continuous improvement include:

- Develop long-term action plans that result in a "built-in" process for improvement.

- Actively involve employees who offer suggestions for improvement and identify potential solutions to problems.

- Ensure that employees adhere to the system, but have flexibility when required.

- Review services provided by, and service standards of, similar groups to determine more appropriate or effective ways of providing service.

- Monitor new developments in service delivery and implementing applicable concepts.

- Make comparisons to similar groups to determine positive or negative effects of proposed improvements.

- Re-evaluate improvements or changes to ensure expected results are achieved.

- Evaluate performance monitoring periodically to ensure that it is objective and that results are accurate.

- Develop a system that initiates a review whenever any significant change is made.

Best Practices for Providing Value-added Service

"Best practices" is the art of creating consistent success. Your professional staff is the cornerstone of success within the organization; they not only represent the company, they *are* the company, and every one of their actions, as well as yours, should reflect the culture and mission of the organization. Consistency is achieved through standardization and the establishment of best practices.

6 Steps to Developing Best Practices

In order to establish best practices for your organization, you need to determine and evaluate current skills, systems, and processes. Unless you establish current levels of performance, best practices become difficult to identify and develop. Here are the six steps to developing best practices:

Step 1: Establish current levels of performance by surveying tenants to determine their level of satisfaction and to assess their future needs.

Step 2: Identify current systems and processes by evaluating their effectiveness and efficiency.

Step 3: Identify strengths and weaknesses within those systems and processes.

Step 4: Create new systems, processes, and skills where necessary.

Step 5: Standardize the systems, skills, or processes.

Step 6: Continuously maintain, innovate, and improve the standard.

Devising Best Practices for Better Customer Service

The following lists are some great examples of "best practices" designed to provide superior customer service and help those organization committed to providing service excellence retain business, brand the level of service they provide, and keep the service promise.

The 6 Steps of Building Tours

The all-important Building Tour, oftentimes a prospect's first experience at the property, will naturally have a lasting impression. From the moment the prospect enters the building, the culture of service, quality, and attention to detail must be experienced. Here are seven steps to providing an excellent building tour, each and every time:

Step 1: A needs analysis will determine the type of tour you have arranged, including having on hand those key individuals who will form the service team for the customer, i.e., the Property Manager, Engineer, Receptionist, Concierge, etc. A quick personal introduction to these members will help establish rapport, and if the prospective customer has any questions, these service team members should be encouraged to speak freely and to be as helpful as possible.

Step 2: The tour begins with someone in the Lobby who greets the customer. In addition, a welcome sign should be posted in the Lobby, such as "ABC Building Welcomes XYZ Corporation!"

Step 3: The tour is conducted at this stage with emphasis on the features and benefits critical to the comfort of the customer, as determined by their needs analysis. Key aspects of the tenant's needs should be fresh in the mind of the agent conducting the tour so he/she can discuss them intimately at this time. This will impress upon the prospect that this is not a "tour by rote," but instead a personalized demonstration of how life at the building can meet their needs.

Step 4: Consider providing on-site CADD (Computer Aided Drafting and Design) services. While this is a labor-intensive process, it will ultimately provide the leasing agents with a state-of-the-art marketing/letting tool that can result in earlier commitment. For instance, at this stage of the building tour, with on-site CADD, it will be possible to visually demonstrate to the customer flexibility of design, rapid development of partition plans, furniture layout, etc. In addition to the service and benefits of CADD to both the customer and the leasing team, this graphically impressive marketing tool entices prospective customers to emotionally commit to the project on the fist tour.

Step 5: Once the tour has concluded, most customers (and agents) expect a summary presentation of the property. At this time, provide the prospective customer or agent with a Features and Benefit Sheet of the building, a Directory of Services, along with the names of key people providing them, and a tasteful gift/memento. An appropriate gift/memento supports the marketing and institutional positioning of the building. It implies high quality standard, reinforces awareness, and keeps the property in the mind of the customer/agent.

Step 6: Follow up contact with each and every customer after the tour. Thank the customer for taking the time to tour the building; provide a package of information that summarizes the customer's needs, the features and benefits of the building, and any other aspect of tenant occupancy discussed during the tour. Take this opportunity to address any unanswered questions and to seek feedback.

10 Added Touches for Building Tours

A successful building tour is a wonderful opportunity to foreshadow your commitment to excellence in customer service. From background music to aesthetics, there are many hidden ways to make a building tour more successful. Here are ten for starters:

- Make sure all plants are watered and trimmed properly

- Make sure lobby ash trays are emptied and brushed
- Make sure the lighting works and is ON when customer arrives
- Make sure the blinds or window treatments are attractive (all blinds open or all shut)
- Make sure the carpet is clean or the bare floors are swept
- Make sure the windows are clean
- Make sure there is no debris in walking tour area
- Make sure the air temperature is suitable for climate/time of year
- Have refreshments available
- Provide background music, if appropriate

5 Things to do When the Tenant Moves In

The process of serving doesn't end when the tenant moves in. In fact, this is just the beginning. To keep a tenant, provide excellent word of mouth through that tenant, and retain building population, excellent customer service must be the letter of the day. What follows is a scenario of the five steps to engage in, through move-in to renewal, including:

- Prior to Occupancy
- Move-In
- Moving Day
- The Next Day
- After Occupancy

2 Steps to Take Prior to Occupancy

Serving can begin even prior to a tenant moving in. Here's how:

- **Team Meets Tenant**: The Property Manager, Leasing Agent, and appropriate specialty staff host an information session at the customer's office prior to lease execution for a preliminary consultation. The purpose of this meeting is to reiterate a clear understanding of the customer's needs and how you can provide for them. If the customer has unique needs, the appropriate representative (specialty staff) must be present to assure the customer that those special needs will be met.

- **Meet with Tenant's Employees**: The Property Manager should be present at the time relocation is announced to customer's staff in order to offer information and answer questions about the building, security, keys, access codes, etc., and to provide a relocation package.

7 Steps to a Flawless Move-In

As you might imagine, relocation is a major disruption to a customer's business operation. Excellent service begins prior to the move by anticipating some of the tenant's immediate needs and providing information and solutions that will assist the customer in planning and coordinating the move. Your foresight will impress the customer and will reinforce the culture of the organization: excellent customer service and attention to detail. Take the following seven steps approximately one week prior to move-in:

- Request a meeting with the customer; include those individuals who will be key customer representatives. Re-introduce the Property Management Team and any other key service team members to the customer.

- Host an information session for customer's staff, most of whom probably have questions about the new building. This is an excellent opportunity to create goodwill by helping the customer educate staff about the building and its operations.

- Explain freight lift bookings, the security system, after-hours parking, after-hours air-conditioning, and the landlord's insurance requirements of the customer for the move.

- Suggest that the moving contractor walk through the building before the move, particularly if the customer is unfamiliar with the building.

- Confirm the customer's new business address.

- Provide the customer with a "Customer Information Directory" that explains the building and services in greater detail.

- Brief your maintenance and security staff so that they are prepared to address any problems or questions the customer might encounter during the move.

2 Steps to a Seamless Moving Day

Take whatever action is necessary to ensure that the move-in is smooth and trouble-free. The following two steps should be at the top of this list:

- Ensure that the freight lift and loading dock are reserved for the customer's exclusive use during the move.

- Make sure that all moving contractors are familiar with the layout of the site and the operation of the lifts ahead of time.

2 Steps for the Next Day

Just because the tenant has moved in doesn't mean the adjustment period is over—or that numerous opportunities to serve have passed you by. Here are two priceless ways to show how much you care the day after a tenant has moved in:

- It should become mandatory practice to visit new customers on their first day to verify that the move went smoothly, to answer questions, and to say, in general, "Welcome to the building."

- It should be standard practice to welcome new customers with a gift on the first day. For example, send an arrangement of flowers for the reception area and/or provide morning tea and refreshments to the staff.

What to do After Occupancy

Wondering how to continue your flawless move-in service after the dust has settled and the tenant's gone back to work? A luncheon is the perfect opportunity for the Property Management and Staff to meet the Customer, if they haven't already done so.

Within two to three day of occupancy, Management should invite the customer's key staff members, those with whom Management and Staff will most likely interact on a regular basis, for a luncheon/breakfast type gathering. This puts a face to the voice on the telephone and, consequently, personalizes service. In addition, it is important to encourage feedback regarding service at this stage.

12 Great Ideas for a Tenant Luncheon

Lunch is served! But just like a meal, there are as many ways to serve lunch as there are guests to enjoy it. Here are fifteen of our favorite ideas for the "after move in" luncheon:

- A sundae bar
- Old-fashioned hot dog stand
- Do-it-yourself hamburgers
- Salad bar
- Pasta bar
- Taco bar
- Chinese buffet
- Picnic lunch
- Outdoor barbecue
- Buffet line
- Brunch
- Breakfast

Perfecting Best Practices:

The 8 Principles of Continuous Improvement

Continuously improving your quality service department requires constant attention and respect. To achieve this miraculous feat, here are eight principles of continuous improvement:

- **Focus on the customers**. When the customer is the focus, the focus is on target. Always.

- **Make improvements unceasingly**. Never stop improving. Learn from your mistakes, learn from tenants, learn from classes, learn from books, learn from tapes, just never stop learning—to improve.

- **Acknowledge problems openly**. A problem won't go away just because you cover it up. Don't blame, hide, or lie. Admit defeat and move on—with a proven solution.

- **Stress teamwork**. You can't do it all yourself, nor should you. Work as a team at improving, and share the duties—as well as the wealth.

- **Develop self-discipline**. Start with your self. Continuously improve, and demand the same from your coworkers and staff.

- **Inform every staff member**. Through meetings, memos, Emails, and informal discussions, inform your staff member of steps you're taking for continuous improvement.

- **Enable every staff member**. Don't just tell your staff what to do, give them the tools to do it.

- **Recruit the right individuals**. Develop a winning team and, as appropriate, add to that winning team with more winners. (See list on the next page for how!)

9 Characteristics of the Ideal Recruit

Providing consistent, reliable, quality service depends upon a staff of the very best recruits in the market. It is impossible to *manage* effectively without *hiring* effectively. The goal is to hire an individual with the personality and service-minded disposition necessary to provide excellent customer service. Here are eight qualities you should be looking for in such a recruit:

- Motivated
- Self-directed
- Relationship oriented
- Team player
- Service minded
- Technical knowledge or aptitude for same
- Approachable and confident
- Attention to detail
- Willing to improve—continuously

5 Tips for Retaining Quality Employees

Providing quality customer service isn't a one-man or one-woman job anymore. Far from it! Nowadays, it requires a full team of trained professionals who hang around long enough to buy into the company visions and gain empowerment through loyal support. Here are five tips for retaining such high-quality employees within your organization:

- **Offer a Vision**: Employees are much more likely to stick around if they feel ownership of the company they work for. This requires a shared vision for the future between employer and employees.

- **Stress Team Play**: Don't make power plays, make *team* plays. Constant teamwork is an important factor in quality employee retention.

- **Empower Employees**: Give employees the power to make their own decisions by training them properly in the reasons behind good customer service—and not just the service standards.

- **Measure and Reward Excellent Service**: Never give blanket congratulations to your entire organization. Those who didn't earn it won't benefit, and those that did will fume. Make note of measurable performance standards and reward those individuals who meet—or exceed—your expectations.

- **Listen to your Employees**: Perhaps the easiest task on this list is to simply hear your employees out. Whether individually or collectively, make it known that your door is open—and use it to welcome in employees both frustrated and favorite.

5 Ways to Improve Internal Customer Service

Customer service begins inside—where it counts. If you can't practice it inside, chances are you won't be practicing it outside either. Here are five great ways to improve internal customer service and set the pattern from the inside:

- Develop Standard Operating Procedures

- Cross-train all employees involved in the process

- Provide an open workspace which is conducive to effective communication

- Leverage technology to network systems—share documents and data

- Communicate frequently

The 5 Traits of Ongoing Customer Relations

Ongoing customer relations equals tenant retention. It's a simple formula and, in black and white, just as easy as that. In real life, of course, we all know how things can pop up to cause a tenant to be dissatisfied. When they do, here are five steps that will help increase ongoing customer relations:

- Practice consistent, reliable, ongoing customer service.

- Ensure that all staff understand the culture of the organization and their obligations to the customer.

- Reinforce the ten essential attitude shifts for improving service quality, as well as the mission statement; let customers dictate the level of service.

- Provide the "small things" for your customers.

- "Small things" say to the tenant/customer/employee "we care" and demonstrate value and attention to detail.

Michael J. Lipsey

Complaint Management

Every complaint, service request, or problem is an opportunity to serve your customer, improve the service, and build customer loyalty. Effective complaint management is a systematic process that includes discovery, confirmation, and resolution. The goal is to keep a minor error/complaint from becoming a major confrontation. Your ability to manage the inevitable problems is the real test of good customer service.

Every employee or representative who comes in contact with the tenant will eventually be approached with a query, complaint, or request for service. The ability to respond to that tenant is the point at which our service culture and reputation will be measured. It is therefore critical that all employees know how to manage and respond to complaints from tenants.

Complaint Management begins with the manner in which we respond to the tenant. When dealing face-to-face it is important to remember that how we project ourselves outweighs what we say or how we say it.

Tone of voice becomes very important when dealing with customers over the phone. The philosophy is that every complaint, service request, or problem is an opportunity to serve our tenants, improve the level of service, and build tenant loyalty.

8 Types of Complainers

Like children on a playground, complaints come in all shapes and sizes. *Unlike* children on a playground, complaints are rarely "fun." To better prepare yourself for the kinds of complaints that happen most in commercial real estate, here are eight types of complainers, and how best to deal with them:

- **The constant whiner**: This one's pretty self-explanatory. Nothing's ever right, and even when it is, they'll find something to whine about. The best way to treat a constant whiner is to be a constant fixer, applying the general rules and standards of service for each and every complaint—individually.

- **The aggressive bully**: Don't take bullies personally, and know that this personality type is the same at a restaurant, at a ball game, at a friend's party. Be consistent in your complaint management, respectful in your personal dealings, and always count to ten before answering.

- **The "Everything's fine, but…"**: This giver of mixed signals merely wants some attention, and you'll often find that the complaint is minor, if justifiable at all. Fix it with kindness, and everything will be fine.

- **The "One small favor…"**: This type of complainer rarely has anything specific to request, except for "favors." These favors come in the form of small requests, which if granted individually, on a consistent basis, will always keep you out of trouble.

- **The buddy**: Beware of "the buddy." The buddy will wear you down with constant requests, and is often a combination of all of the above! Treat your buddy like a distant friend, responding promptly to formal requests, and asking for formal requests when given a hint.

- **The enemy**: The enemy comes off strong and stays that way. His goal is to get the most he can, for little return, and keep getting it until he can't get it anymore. Be as firm as possible with this tenant, and kill him with kindness.

- **The warrior**: The warrior is always out for a battle, loaded for bear, etc. The best thing to do here is be prepared with written complaint forms and how they were handled to plead your case when he—eventually—complains to higher-ups.

- **The losing battle**: Every building has a tenant that qualifies as a "losing battle." One who rarely pays on time, but is prompt to complain. When the complaints get too big, and the payments too small, it is best to cut this tenant and make space available for someone more deserving—and forthright with their payments!

4 Components of Complaint Management

There is no customer service task more daunting than the onus of complaint management. Customer complaints often lead to heated tempers, and it is important for you—and your staff—to take the high road at such times and remain calm and cool. To assist you, here are the four components of complaint management:

- **Listen:** Learning to listen is critical. See the following page for the three essential steps of the listening process.

- **Accept Responsibility:** While it is difficult to listen to a complaint, it is important to accept that the tenant is not happy and something must be done. If possible offer an immediate solution, if not a complete resolution.

- **Apologize:** No matter how hard it is, or whose fault it was, or the circumstances, always apologize to the tenant for any inconvenience.

- **Fix it . . . and More**: Apologizing, however, is never enough. Fixing the problem is the only resolution, and the only solution a tenant will accept.

Complaints: *3 Steps of the Listening Process*

If you listen effectively, you can gauge the emotional investment in the problem. The following are the three steps of the listening process.

- **LISTEN:** Listen to what the tenant is saying—ask questions and gather as much information regarding the specifics of the complaint.

- **INFORM:** Inform the tenant that their complaint will be entered into the Work Order Response System and provide a timeline for the initial response.

- **ACT:** Find ways to continue to provide the tenant with value during the course of the phone call or communication.

2 Ways to "Fix it . . . and More"

Consider the following benchmarks in our industry from two separate companies each with their own complaint management standard:

Case #1:

ABC Management is based in Boston, with properties in South Carolina and Washington, DC. When air-conditioning equipment breakdowns occur in their buildings, they provide portable fans on loan to tenants, with an apology.

Case #2:

If the air conditioning breaks down in a building managed by XYZ Commercial Real Estate Services in Florida, Haagen-Dazs ice cream and sodas are delivered to each tenant as a "pardon the inconvenience" gesture. This assures the tenants that management is "on their side" and on top of the problem.

Service Recovery

> *"The word 'recovery' has been chosen carefully. It means 'to return to a normal state; to make whole again.' Though many organizations have service departments established to fix what breaks, the deliberate management of the recovery is typically a reactive, damage-minimizing function. We suggest recovery can be as proactively managed for positive outcomes as can service in general."*
>
> **—Chip Bell and Ron Zemke**, *Management Review*

6 Steps to Service Recovery

Most managers are not prepared to *delight* tenants who need maintenance in their leased space. Instead, managers tend to "over-promise and under-deliver," a practice that leads to distrust and a loss of credibility. *Never* promise what cannot be delivered. Most firms fail to understand the importance of managing customer expectations. To achieve that feat, her are the six steps to service recovery:

- **Apologize**: It does not matter who was at fault; apologize and show concern.

- **Listen and Empathize**: Show customers you care about the issue.

- **Fix the Problem Quickly and Fairly**: Give the customer what was expected in the first place—and do it promptly.

- **Offer Atonement**: Offer a value-added gesture as compensation.

- **Keep Promises**: Especially those made during the recovery phase.

- **Follow-up**: As soon as possible, ascertain customer satisfaction.

Understanding Emotional Escalation

What happens to the client's emotional state when expectations are not met and the customer becomes emotionally invested in the problem? Your immediate goal is to listen and respond so that you can bring the customer anger down to a level at which you can negotiate. If you allow the call to end without resolution, or at least a solution or plan of action that satisfies the tenant, emotions will escalate and you begin to lose credibility.

Level	Emotion	Expectation
One	Frustration	Fault to report – it will be taken care of with one phone call
Two	Disappointment	Unresolved after first call – Customer places second call
Three	Anger	Unresolved with no information as to why – Customer demands action – all credibility is lost

(**Source**: *Technical Assistance Research Programs Institute*)

10 Signs of Emotional Escalation

Emotional escalation can be the death knell of solid customer service. When can you tell that your tenant's emotions are starting to escalate? Simple. Check for the following ten signs of emotional escalation:

- Loud voice
- Hostile body language
- Verbal threats
- Coarse language

- Physical proximity
- Rising color
- Fidgeting
- Exaggerated mannerisms
- Frantic gestures
- Pointing

"Our Customers Never Complain"

Be wary of customers who never complain—an absence of complaints may mean that the company is out of touch with its customers. The consequences will be dire. The firm will almost certainly continue to lose more of its current clientele—without knowing why—and will likely forfeit additional business with potential customers because of negative word of mouth.

Because complaints often identify voids in current services provided, complaint management can become part of a larger process of staying in touch with customers. Feedback from surveys provides and inexpensive and continuous source from which improvements can be made and new services can be offered.

5 Ways to Solicit Complaints

On the other hand, soliciting customer complaints can provide many benefits and opportunities. It provides managers with an excellent way to evaluate their service and assess the level of customer satisfaction. Here are five ways to solicit customer complaints:

- Comment cards
- Suggestion box
- Complaints@abccompany.com
- Complaint form in company newsletter
- 1-800-number for complaints

Branding Quality Service

The ability to successfully brand a product or service requires that the product or service be delivered with reliability, with quality, and on a consistent basis. This ensures that a customer receives the promised service or product, on time, regardless of where it is delivered or by whom.

Basic, consistent value, displayed through actions—fulfilling the promise—is what allows consumers to make the correlation between the company name and the product or service being provided. Just as safety is synonymous with Volvo, and Kleenex commonly refers to facial tissue, so can the service you practice and provide become synonymous with the type of space and level of quality you render.

3 Core Disciplines Necessary to Develop Brand

The association of brand with quality is achieved through consistency, and consistency is attained through operational excellence, driven by a set of core value disciplines that should guide the service strategy. Here are the top three core value disciplines:

- **Operational Excellence**: Providing customers with consistent, reliable, seamless service, delivered with minimal difficulty or inconvenience.

- **Product Leadership**: Providing a product/service that continually redefines the state of the art; thinking ahead of the curve.

- **Customer Intimacy**: Providing a proactive approach to customer service. Anticipating customer needs. Selling the customer a total solution—not just a product or service.

The Benefits of Branding Service

Evidence from research consistently shows that reliability is the foremost criterion customers consider in evaluating the quality of a company's service. While reliability is not the sole determinant of developing your brand image, it is central. Achieving competitive advantage through consistent, reliable service is critical to the branding process and can have several significant benefits:

"Operationally excellent companies, those that are able to brand their product, service, and image, run themselves like the Marine Corps: everyone knows the battle plan and the rule book—and when the buzzer sounds, everyone knows exactly what he or she has to do. For operationally excellent companies, a promise is a promise."

—*The Discipline of Operational Excellence*

Sample Letters to *Potential* Tenants

The following sample letters are examples of how to continue to add value and increase the level of customer service while facilitating the day-to-day sale, lease, and management of commercial property. Use them "as is" or customize for your specific tenant or situation:

Thank you for scheduling an appointment

Dear _____,

We are delighted that you have chosen _____ as a possible provider for your company's needs. Our facilities and staff offer numerous unique amenities and services, and we feel certain that we will meet and exceed your expectations. Our company's reputation for quality and excellence is well-recognized in the industry; our tenants come first.

At your scheduled visit on _____ (date) at _____ (time), you will be meeting with _____, whose responsibilities include _____. During your building tour, you will have many opportunities to ask questions and to get a feel for the outstanding value of our services. If questions remain after your tour, or if you have any concerns or additional needs, please give us a call.

We look forward to meeting with you and your representatives next week. If you anticipate any special needs, or have any pre-visit questions or concerns, feel free to contact _____ at _____. Thanks again for choosing to explore our services.

Sincerely,

The Staff of ABC Building

Thank you for your call

Dear _____,

It was a pleasure to talk with you this week when you called to inquire about _____. Your questions are important to us, and we hope that the information that you received satisfied your needs.

If you would like to discuss any further questions, or if you would like to meet with one of our representatives, please give us a call. We offer a full-range of customer service options, and we look forward to any opportunity to serve you.

Sincerely,

The Staff of ABC Building

Thank you for your visit

Dear _____,

Thank you so much for your recent visit to _____ property. It was a pleasure to discuss your organization's needs and the services we offer. As you make your decision, if any questions surface or if you would like to speak with one of our representatives, please give us a call.

We look forward to providing you with customized services of the finest quality at the best possible price. Let us help your organization make this move something to celebrate!

Sincerely,

The Staff of ABC Building

Pre-visit welcome

Dear _____,

We are delighted that you have scheduled a visit to _____ property on _____ (date) at _____ (time). During your tour, you will have many opportunities to ask questions and to get to know our staff. Please feel free to bring a list of questions and concerns; we encourage guests to make a "wish list" of services advantageous to your company.

After your visit, we feel certain you will recognize the outstanding value and service we offer; we look forward to meeting your needs and surpassing your expectations.

Sincerely,

The Staff of ABC Building

Post-visit survey - reaction to our meeting

Dear _____,

We thoroughly enjoyed meeting with you and your representatives when you visited our property last week. Just to make certain that we did our best to provide an informative, congenial visit, we would appreciate your input. If you would contact _____ at _____ with the following information, it will help us continue to provide the very best.

Sincerely,

The Staff of ABC Building

Post-visit Survey

We look forward to your response; your opinion is valuable to us. Best wishes for continued success, and do not hesitate to call if we can provide further service:

1. Did management and staff provide all requested information?

2. Did you feel welcomed and comfortable?

3. Did the facility meet your needs?

4. How well did the visit meet your expectations?

5. How well did our management/staff meet your expectations?

6. How well do our services fit your needs/expectations?

7. What other services might you find helpful?

FYI Courtesy Contact: *Did you know that we offer...*

Dear _____,

If you are considering property options, or will be in the near future, we hope that you will contact _____ at _____ so that we may design the perfect tenant package for you. We are committed to providing the highest possible service at the very best value, and meeting the needs of tenants is our first priority.

Michael J. Lipsey

Consider the outstanding service options available at our property (ies)

- on-site ATM machines
- on-site postal machines
- on-site day-care
- on-site _____

We look forward to hearing from you. We would enjoy providing a complimentary tour or informational meeting at your convenience.

Sincerely,
The Staff of ABC Building

Letters to *New* and *Existing* Tenants

The following sample letters are examples of how to continue to add value and increase the level of customer service while facilitating the day-to-day sale, lease, and management of commercial property. Use them "as is" or customize for your specific tenant or situation:

Welcome to the building

Dear _____,

The entire management team and facility staff of _____ property extends to you our warmest welcome! We are delighted to offer you the highest quality services at the best possible value. If, however, during your transition or occupancy, you have any concerns, please immediately alert _____ at _____, who will promptly respond to your request.

In addition we are pleased to provide this informational summary:

Information regarding building services: (info on parking, security etc.)

Information regarding staff to contact: (names, titles, phone numbers)

Information regarding payment options: (addresses, deadlines, etc)

If you require any additional information or need any further assistance, we are at your service. Again, welcome to our facility!

Sincerely,

The Staff of ABC Building

Thank-you for timely remittance of payments

Dear _____,

We would like to express our thanks to you for your prompt attention to all payment deadlines. Your timely remittance saves our staff time and effort, and we all appreciate your reliable response.

In addition, if you are considering any service upgrades or have any additional questions or concerns, please contact _____ at _____, We value your input.

Sincerely,

The Staff of ABC Building

Thank you for reporting a problem - has it been resolved?

Dear _____,

We regret any inconvenience you experienced as a result of the _____ (problem) you recently reported. Thank you for promptly notifying our staff; we hope that all concerns have been resolved to your satisfaction. If you have any questions about our response, or for assistance with other business needs, please contact _____ at _____.

Your satisfaction is important to us.

Sincerely,

The Staff of ABC Building

Notice of past-due payment - please remit

Dear _____,

We have noticed that a deadline, _____ (date), for payment in full of _____ (amount) for _____ (service provided) has passed; thus, your account is past due.

As a service to our valued tenants, we provide this courtesy reminder. If you have questions regarding this account or feel that you have received this in error, please contact _____ at _____.

If payment has been sent, please disregard; if not, please remit balance.

Sincerely,
The Staff of ABC Building

Congratulations on the anniversary of tenant occupancy

Dear _____,

We are happy to note that today, _____, marks the _____ anniversary of your move-in. This occasion offers us an opportunity to let you know that we appreciate your occupancy and to express our desire that you feel fully satisfied with our service.

Remember, we can provide expanded options tailored to your needs. Contact _____ at _____ if you would like more details.

Sincerely,
The Staff of ABC Building

Thank you for your collaboration

Dear _____,

We want to express our thanks for your_____
(efficient/innovative/productive) participation at last week's _____
(meeting/work session). The results of our enjoyable collaboration will be
of great benefit. (specify, if possible)

At our next meeting, on _____ (date) at _____ (time) we hope
to discuss _____. (summarize topics) We look forward to our
continued conversations.

Sincerely,

The Staff of ABC Building

Looking forward to our meeting

Dear _____,

We anticipate with pleasure your upcoming appointment on _____
(date) at _____ (time). This meeting offers an opportunity for us to
_____ (share ideas/explore possibilities/clarify issues). We will
provide _____ (snacks/notes/handouts) but you will need to bring
_____ (if applicable).

If you have any immediate questions or concerns, please contact
_____ at _____. We look forward to seeing you soon.

Sincerely,

The Staff of ABC Building

Thank you for seeing our input

Dear _____,

It was a pleasure to provide you with _____ (ideas/services) last week. We value this opportunity for collaboration and hope that you found the _____ (information/service) satisfactory.

If we can be of any other service to you in your endeavors, please contact _____ at _____.

Sincerely,
The Staff of ABC Building

Thank you for introducing others to our services

Dear _____,

We want to send to you our sincere thanks for the positive mention of our services that you made to _____. The courtesy is appreciated; we will do our best to meet (and exceed) all expectations.

If we can ever provide services to you or any other of your associates, please contact _____ at _____.

Sincerely,
The Staff of ABC Building

Congratulations on business anniversary, positive reviews, expansion

Dear _____,

Congratulations! We are pleased to note that you _____ (have been recognized/are celebrating/have just opened) _____ (event). It is a pleasure to share our joy with you on this happy occasion.

We wish you continued success.

Sincerely,

The Staff of ABC Building

Thank You from The Lipsey Company

Dear Friends, Clients and Acquaintances:

It has been our pleasure to serve your training and consulting needs throughout the years.

We have been fortunate to develop many wonderful relationships along the way and look forward to continuing to work with your outstanding companies, organizations and associations in the future.

It is our sincerest hope that our *Systems for Success,* in some small way, contributes to your own continued success in commercial real estate.

Sincerely,

Michael J. Lipsey
President
CCIM, CRB, CPM, MCR